THE *Dairyman's Daughter*

GREAT CHRISTIAN BOOKS
LINDENHURST, NEW YORK

THE *Dairyman's Daughter*

LEGH RICHMOND

A GREAT CHRISTIAN BOOKS publication
Great Christian Books is an imprint of Rotolo Media
160 37th Street Lindenhurst, New York 11757
www.greatchristianbooks.com   (631) 956-0998
email: mail@greatchristianbooks.com
The Dairyman's Daughter
ISBN 978-1-61010-175-2

Richmond, Legh, 1772-1827
The Dairyman's Daughter / by Legh Richmond
p. cm.
A "A Great Christian Book" book
GREAT CHRISTIAN BOOKS an imprint of Rotolo Media
ISBN 978-1-61010-175-2
Recommended Dewey Decimal Classifications: 200, 204, 240
Suggested Subject Headings:
1. Religion—Christianity—Christian moral & devotional theology
2. Religious experience, life & practice
3. Christianity—The Bible—Biographical
I. Title

Book and cover design for this title are by Michael Rotolo. Body text is typeset in the Minion typeface by Adobe Inc. and is manufactured in the United States on acid-free paper. To discuss the publication of your Christian manuscript or out-of-print book, please contact Great Christian Books through www.greatchristianbooks.com.

MANUFACTURED IN THE UNITED STATES OF AMERICA

CONTENTS

CHAPTER ONE

It is a delightful employment to discover and trace the operations of Divine grace, as they are manifested in the dispositions and lives of God's real children. It is peculiarly gratifying to observe how frequently, among the poorer classes of mankind, the sunshine of mercy beams upon the heart, and bears witness to the image of Christ which the Spirit of God has impressed thereupon. Among such, the sincerity and simplicity of the Christian character appear unencumbered by those obstacles to spirituality of mind and conversation, which too often prove a great hindrance to those who live in the higher ranks. Many are the difficulties which riches, worldly consequence, high connections, and the luxuriant refinements of polished society, throw in the way of religious profession. Happy indeed it is (and some such happy instances I know), where grace has so strikingly supported its conflict with natural pride, self-importance, the allurements of luxury, ease, and worldly opinion, that the noble and mighty appear adorned with genuine poverty of spirit, self-denial, humble-mindedness, and deep spirituality of heart.

But in general, if we want to see religion in its most simple and pure character, we must look for it among the poor of this world, who are rich in faith. How often is the poor man's cottage the palace of God! Many can truly declare, that they have there learned the most valuable lessons of faith and hope, and there witnessed the most striking demonstrations of the wisdom, power, and goodness of God.

The character which the present narrative is designed to introduce to the notice of my readers, is given from real life and circumstance. I first became acquainted with her by receiving the following letter, which I transcribe from the original now before me:—

"Rev. Sir,

I take the liberty to write to you. Pray excuse me, for I have never spoken to you. But I once heard you when you preached at—Church. I believe you are a faithful preacher, to warn sinners to flee from the wrath that will be revealed against all those that live in sin, and die impenitent. Pray go on in the strength of the Lord. And may He bless you, and crown your labor of love with success, and give you souls for your hire.

The Lord has promised to be with those whom He calls and sends forth to preach his Word to the end of time: for without Him we can do nothing. I was much rejoiced to hear of those marks of love and affection to that poor soldier of the S. D. Militia. Surely the love of Christ sent you to that poor man! May that love ever dwell richly in you by faith! May it constrain you to seek the wandering souls of men with the fervent desire to spend and be spent for his glory! May the unction of the Holy Spirit attend the word spoken by you with power, and convey deep conviction to the hearts of your hearers! May many of them experience the Divine change of being made new creatures in Christ!

Sir, be fervent in prayer with God for the conviction and conversion of sinners. His power is great, and who can withstand it? He has promised to answer the prayer of faith, that is put up in his Son's name: 'Ask what ye will, it shall be granted you.' How this should strengthen our faith, when we are taught by the Word and the Spirit how to pray! Oh that sweet inspiring hope! how it lifts up the fainting spirits, when we look over the precious promises of God! What a mercy if we know Christ, and the power of his resurrection in our own hearts! Through faith in Christ we rejoice in hope, and look in expectation of that time drawing near, when all shall know and fear the Lord, and when a nation shall be born in a day.

What a happy time when Christ's kingdom shall come! then shall 'his will be done in earth, as it is in heaven.' Men shall be daily fed with the manna of his love, and delight themselves in the Lord all the day long. Then, what a paradise below they will enjoy! How it animates and enlivens my soul with vigour to pursue the ways of God, that I may even now bear some humble part in giving glory to God and the Lamb!

Sir, I began to write this on Sunday, being detained from attending on public worship. My dear and only sister, living as a servant with Mrs—, was so ill that I came here to attend in her place and on her. But now she is no more.

I was going to entreat you to write to her in answer to this, she being convinced of the evil of her past life, and that she had not walked in the ways of God, nor sought to please Him. But she earnestly desired to do so. This makes me have a comfortable hope that she is gone to glory, and that she is now joining in sweet concert with the angelic host in heaven to sing the wonders of redeeming love. I hope I may now write, 'Blessed are the dead which die in the Lord.'

She expressed a desire to receive the Lord's Supper, and commemorate his precious death and sufferings. I told her, as well as I was able, what it was to receive Christ into her heart; but as her weakness of body increased, she did not mention it again. She seemed quite resigned before she died. I do hope she is gone from a world of death and sin, to be with God forever.

Sir, I hope you will not be offended with me, a poor ignorant person, to take such a liberty as to write to you. But I trust, as you are called to instruct sinners in the ways of God, you will bear with me, and be so kind to answer this wrote letter, and give me some instructions. It is my heart's desire to have the mind that was in Christ, that when I awake up in his likeness, then I may be satisfied.

My sister expressed a wish that you might bury her. The minister of our parish, whither she will be carried, cannot come. She will lie at—. She died on Tuesday morning, and will be buried on Friday, or Saturday (whichever is most convenient to you), at three o'clock in the afternoon. Please to send an answer by the bearer, to let me know whether you can comply with this request,

From your unworthy servant,

Elizabeth Wallbridge"

I was much struck with the simple and earnest strain of devotion which this letter breathed. It was but indifferently written and spelt; but this rather tended to endear the hitherto unknown writer, as it seemed characteristic of the union of humbleness of station with eminence of piety. I felt quite thankful that I was favoured with a correspondent of this description; the more so, as such characters were at this time very rare in the neighbourhood. I have often wished that epistolary intercourse of this kind was more encouraged and practised among us. I have the greatest reason to speak well of its effect, both on myself and others. Communication by letter as well as by conversation with the pious poor, has often been the instrument of animating and reviving my own heart in the midst of duty, and of giving me the most profitable information for the general conduct of the ministerial office.

As soon as the letter was read, I inquired who was the bearer of it.

"He is waiting at the outside of the gate, sir," was the reply.

I went out to speak to him, and saw a venerable old man, whose long hoary hair and deeply-wrinkled countenance commanded more than common respect. He was resting his arm upon the gate, and tears were streaming down his cheeks. On my approach he made a low bow, and said:

"Sir, I have brought you a letter from my daughter; but I fear you will think us very bold in asking you to take so much trouble."

"By no means," I replied; "I shall be truly glad to oblige you and any of your family in this matter, provided it be quite agreeable to the minister of your parish."

"Sir, he told me yesterday that he should be very glad if I could procure some gentleman to come and bury my poor child for him, as he lives five miles off, and has particular business on that day. So, when I told my daughter, she asked me to come to you, sir, and bring that letter, which would explain the matter."

I desired him to come into the house, and then said:

"What is your occupation?"

"Sir, I have lived most of my days in a little cottage at—, six miles from here. I have rented a few acres of ground, and kept some cows, which, in addition to my day-labor, has been the means of supporting and bringing up my family."

"What family have you?"

"A wife, now getting very aged and helpless, two sons and one daughter; for my other poor dear child is just departed out of this wicked world."

"I hope for a better."

"I hope so, too, poor thing. She did not use to take to such good ways as her sister; but I do believe that her sister's manner of talking with her before she died, was the means of saving her soul. What a mercy it is to have such a child as mine is! I never thought about my own soul seriously till she, poor girl, begged and prayed me to flee from the wrath to come."

"How old are you?"

"Near seventy, and my wife is older; we are getting old, and almost past our labor, but our daughter has left a good place, where she lived in service, on purpose to come home and take care of us and our little dairy. And a dear, dutiful, affectionate girl she is."

"Was she always so?"

"No, sir: when she was very young, she was all for the world, and pleasure, and dress, and company. Indeed, we were all very ignorant, and thought if we took care for this life, and wronged nobody, we should be sure to go to heaven at last. My daughters were both wilful, and, like ourselves, strangers to the ways of God and the Word of his grace. But the eldest of them went out to service, and some years ago she heard a sermon at—Church, by a gentleman that was going to—, as chaplain to the colony; and from that time she seemed quite another creature. She began to read the Bible, and became sober and steady. The first time she returned home afterwards to see us, she brought us a guinea which she had saved from her wages, and said, as we were getting old, she was sure we should want help; adding, that she did not wish to spend it in fine clothes, as she used to do, only to feed pride and vanity. She said she would rather show gratitude to her dear father and mother, because Christ had shown such mercy to her.

"We wondered to hear her talk, and took great delight in her company; for her temper and behavior were so humble and kind, she seemed so desirous to do us good both in soul and body, and was so different from what we had ever seen before, that, careless and ignorant as we had been, we began to think there must be something real in religion, or it never could alter a person so much in a little time.

"Her youngest sister, poor soul! used to laugh and ridicule her at that time, and said her head was turned with her new ways. 'No, sister,' she would say; 'not my head, but I hope my heart is turned from the love of sin to the love of God. I wish you may one day see, as I do, the danger and vanity of your present condition.'

"Her poor sister would reply, 'I do not want to hear any of your preaching; I am no worse than other people, and that is enough for me.'

"'Well, sister,' Elizabeth would say, 'if you will not

hear me, you cannot hinder me from praying for you, which I do with all my heart.'

"And now, sir, I believe those prayers are answered. For when her sister was taken ill, Elizabeth went to Mrs—'s to wait in her place, and take care of her. She said a great deal to her about her soul, and the poor girl began to be so deeply affected, and sensible of her past sin, and so thankful for her sister's kind behaviour, that it gave her great hopes indeed for her sake. When my wife and I went to see her, as she lay sick, she told us how grieved and ashamed she was of her past life, but said she had a hope through grace that her sister's Savior would be her Savior too; for she saw her own sinfulness, felt her own helplessness, and only wished to cast herself upon Christ as her hope and salvation.

"And now, sir, she is gone; and I hope and think her sister's prayers for her conversion to God have been answered. The Lord grant the same for her poor father and mother's sake likewise!"

This conversation was a very pleasing commentary upon the letter which I had received, and made me anxious both to comply with the request, and to become acquainted with the writer. I promised the good Dairyman to attend on the Friday at the appointed hour; and after some more conversation respecting his own state of mind under the present trial, he went away.

He was a reverend old man; his furrowed cheeks, white locks, weeping eyes, bent shoulders, and feeble gait, were characteristic of the aged pilgrim. As he slowly walked onwards, supported by a stick which seemed to have been the companion of many a long year, a train of reflections occurred, which I retrace with pleasure and emotion.

At the appointed hour I arrived at the church, and after a little while was summoned to the churchyard gate to meet the funeral procession. The aged parents, the elder brother, and the sister, with other relatives, formed an affecting group. I was struck with the humble, pious, and pleasing countenance of the young woman from whom I had received the letter. It bore the marks of great seriousness without affectation, and of much serenity mingled with a glow of devotion.

A circumstance occurred during the reading of the burial service, which I think it right to mention, as one among many testimonies of the solemn and impressive tendency of our truly evangelical Liturgy.

A man of the village, who had hitherto been of a very careless and even profligate character, went into the church through mere curiosity, and with no better purpose than that of vacantly gazing at the ceremony. He came likewise to the grave, and, during the reading of those prayers which are appointed for that part of the service, his mind received a deep, serious conviction of his sin and spiritual danger. It was an impression that never wore off, but gradually ripened into the most satisfactory evidence of an entire change, of which I had many and long-continued proofs. He always referred to the burial service, and to some particular sentences of it, as the clearly ascertained instrument of bringing him, through grace, to the knowledge of the truth.

The day was therefore one to be remembered. Remembered let it be by those who love to hear

"The short and simple annals of the poor."

Was there not a manifest and happy connection between the circumstances that providentially brought the serious and the careless to the same grave on that day together? How much do they lose who neglect to trace the leadings of God in providence, as links in the chain of his eternal purpose of redemption and grace!

"While infidels may scoff, let us adore."

After the service was concluded, I had a short conversation with the good old couple and their daughter. She had told me that she intended to remain a week or two at the gentleman's house where her sister died, till another servant should arrive and take her sister's place.

"I shall be truly obliged," said she, "by an opportunity of conversing with you, either there or at my father's, when I return home, which will be in the course of a fortnight at the farthest. I shall be glad to talk to you about my sister, whom you have just buried."

Her aspect and address were highly interesting. I promised to see her very soon; and then returned home, quietly reflecting on the circumstances of the funeral at which I had been engaged. I blessed the God of the poor; and prayed that the poor might become rich in faith, and the rich be made poor in spirit.

CHAPTER TWO

A sweet solemnity often possesses the mind, whilst retracing past intercourse with departed friends. How much is this increased, when they were such as lived and died in the Lord! The remembrance of former scenes and conversations with those who, we believe, are now enjoying the uninterrupted happiness of a better world, fills the heart with pleasing sadness, and animates the soul with the hopeful anticipation of a day when the glory of the Lord shall be revealed in the assembling of all his children together, never more to be separated. Whether they were rich or poor while on earth, is a matter of trifling consequence; the valuable part of their character is, that they are kings and priests unto God, and this is their true nobility. In the number of now departed believers, with whom I once loved to converse on the grace and glory of the kingdom of God, was the Dairyman's daughter.

About a week after the funeral I went to visit the family at—, in whose service the youngest sister had lived and died, and where Elizabeth was requested to remain for a short time in her stead.

The house was a large and venerable mansion. It stood in a beautiful valley at the foot of a high hill. It was embowered in fine woods, which were interspersed in every direction with rising, falling, and swelling grounds. The manor-house had evidently descended through a long line of ancestry, from a distant period of time. The Gothic character of its original architecture was still preserved in the latticed windows, adorned with carved divisions and pillars of stone-work. Several pointed terminations also, in the construction of the roof, according to the custom of our forefathers, fully corresponded with the general features of the building.

One end of the house was entirely clothed with the thick foliage of an immense ivy, which climbed beyond customary limits, and embraced a lofty chimney up to its very summit. Such a tree seemed congenial to the walls that supported it, and conspired with the antique fashion of the place to carry imagination back to the days of our ancestors.

As I approached, I was led to reflect on the lapse of ages, and the successive generations of men, each in their turn occupying lands, houses, and domains; each in their turn also disappearing, and leaving their inheritance to be enjoyed by others. David once observed the same, and cried out, "Behold, thou hast made my days as an hand-breadth, and mine age is as nothing before thee: verily every man at his best state is altogether vanity. Surely every man walketh in a vain show; surely they are disquieted in vain: he heapeth up riches, and knoweth not who shall gather them." (Ps. 39:5,6)

Happy would it be for the rich, if they more frequently meditated on the uncertainty of all their possessions, and the frail nature of every earthly tenure. "Their inward thought is, that their houses shall continue forever, and their dwelling-places to all generations: they call their lands after their own names. Nevertheless, man being in honor abideth not: he is like the beasts that perish. This their way is their folly; yet their posterity approve their sayings. Like sheep they are laid in the grave; death shall feed on them; and their beauty shall consume in the grave from their dwelling." (Ps. 49:11-14)

As I advanced to the mansion, a pleasing kind of gloom overspread the front: it was occasioned by the shade of trees, and gave a characteristic effect to the ancient fabric. I instantly recollected that death had very recently visited the house, and that one of its present inhabitants was an affectionate mourner for a departed sister.

There is a solemnity in the thought of a recent death which will associate itself with the very walls, from whence we are conscious that a soul has just taken its flight to eternity.

After passing some time in conversation with the superiors of the family, in the course of which I was much gratified by hearing of the unremitted attention which the elder sister had paid to the younger during the illness of the latter. I received likewise other testimonies of the excellency of her general character and conduct in the house. I then took leave, requesting permission to see her, agreeably to the promise I had made at the funeral, not many days before.

I was shown into a parlour, where I found her alone. She was in deep mourning. She had a calmness and serenity in her countenance, which exceedingly struck me, and impressed some idea of those attainments which a further acquaintance with her afterwards so much increased.

She spoke of her sister. I had the satisfaction of finding that she had given very hopeful proofs of a change of heart before she died. The prayers and earnest exhortations of Elizabeth had been blessed to a happy effect. She described what had passed with such a mixture of sisterly affection and pious dependence on the mercy of God to sinners, as convinced me that her own heart was under the influence of "pure and undefiled religion."

She requested leave occasionally to correspond with me on serious subjects, stating that she needed much instruction. She hoped I would pardon the liberty which she had taken by introducing herself to my notice. She expressed a trust that the Lord would overrule both the death of her sister and the personal acquaintance with me that resulted from it, to a present and future good, as it respected herself and also her parents, with whom she statedly lived, and to whom she expected to return in a few days.

Finding that she was wanted in some household duty, I did not remain long with her, but left her with an assurance that I proposed to visit her parents very shortly.

"Sir," said she, "I take it very kind that you have condescended to leave the company of the rich and converse with the poor. I wish I could have said more to you respecting my own state of mind. Perhaps I shall be better able another time. When you next visit me, instead of finding me in these noble walls, you will see me in a poor cottage. But I am happiest when there. Once more, sir, I thank you for your past kindness to me and mine, and may God in many ways bless you for it."

I quitted the house with no small degree of satisfaction, in consequence of the new acquaintance which I had formed. I discovered traces of a cultivated as well as a spiritual mind. I felt that religious intercourse with those of low estate may be rendered eminently useful to others, whose outward station and advantages are far above their own.

How often does it appear that "God hath chosen the weak things of the world to confound the things which are mighty; and base things of the world, and things which are despised, hath God chosen, yea, and things which are not, to bring to nought things that are: that no flesh should glory in his presence." (1 Cor. 1:27-29)

It was not infrequently my custom, when my mind was filled with any interesting subject for meditation, to seek some spot where the beauties of natural prospect might help to form pleasing and useful associations. I therefore ascended gradually to the very summit of the hill adjoining the mansion where my visit had just been made. Here was placed an elevated sea mark: it was in the form of a triangular pyramid, and built of stone. I sat down on the ground near it, and looked at the surrounding prospect, which was distinguished for beauty and magnificence. It was a lofty station, which commanded a complete circle of interesting objects to engage the spectator's attention.

Southward the view was terminated by a long range of hills, at about six miles distance. They met, to the westward, another chain of hills, of which the one whereon I sat formed a link; and the whole together nearly encompassed a rich and fruitful valley, filled with cornfields and pastures. Through this vale winded a small river for many miles: much cattle were feeding on its banks. Here and there lesser eminences arose in the valley, some covered with wood, others with corn or grass, and a few with heath or fern. One of these little hills was distinguished by a parish church at the top, presenting a striking feature in the landscape. Another of these elevations, situated in the centre of the valley, was adorned with a venerable holly tree, which had grown there for ages. Its singular height and wide-spreading dimensions not only render it an object of curiosity to the traveller, but of daily usefulness to the pilot, as a mark visible from the sea, whereby to direct his vessel safe into harbour. Villages, churches, country-seats, farm-houses, and cottages were scattered over every part of the southern valley. In this direction, also, at the foot of the hill where I was stationed, appeared the ancient mansion, which I had just quitted, embellished with its woods, groves, and gardens.

South-eastward, I saw the open ocean, bounded only by the horizon. The sun shone, and gilded the waves with a glittering light that sparkled in the most brilliant manner. More to the east, in continuation of that line of hills where I was placed, rose two downs, one beyond the other, both covered with sheep, and the sea just visible over the farthest of them, as a terminating boundary. In this point ships were seen, some sailing, others at anchor. Here the little river, which watered the southern valley, finished its course, and ran through meadows into the sea, in an eastward direction.

On the north the sea appeared like a noble river, varying from three to seven miles in breadth, between the banks of the opposite coast and those of the island which I inhabited. Immediately underneath me was a fine woody district of country, diversified by many pleasing objects. Distant towns were visible on the opposite shore. Numbers of ships occupied the sheltered station which this northern channel afforded them. The eye roamed with delight over an expanse of near and remote beauties, which alternately caught the observation, and which harmonised together, and produced a scene of peculiar interest.

Westward, the hills followed each other, forming several intermediate and partial valleys, in a kind of undulations, like the waves of the sea, and, bending to the south, completed the boundary of the larger valley before described, to the southward of the hill on which I sat. In many instances the hills were cultivated with corn to their very summits, and seemed to defy the inclemency of weather, which, at these heights, usually renders the ground incapable of bringing forth and ripening the crops of grain. One hill alone, the highest in elevation, and about ten miles to the south-westward, was enveloped in a cloud, which just permitted a dim and hazy sight of a signal-post, a lighthouse, and an ancient chantry, built on its summit.

Amidst these numerous specimens of delightful scenery I found a mount for contemplation, and here I indulged it.

"How much of the natural beauties of Paradise still remain in the world, although its spiritual character has been so awfully defaced by sin! But when Divine grace renews the heart of the fallen sinner, Paradise is regained, and much of its beauty restored to the soul. As this prospect is compounded of hill and dale, land and sea, woods and plains, all sweetly blended together and relieving each other in the landscape; so do the gracious dispositions wrought in the soul produce a beauty and harmony of scene to which it was before a stranger."

I looked towards the village in the plain below, where the Dairyman's younger daughter was buried. I retraced the simple solemnities of the funeral. I connected the principles and conduct of her sister with the present probably happy state of her soul in the world of spirits, and was greatly impressed with a sense of the importance of family influence as a means of grace. "That young woman," I thought, "has been the conductor of not only a sister, but, perhaps, a father and mother also, to the true knowledge of God, and may, by Divine blessing, become so to others. It is a glorious occupation to win souls to Christ, and guide them out of Egyptian bondage through the wilderness into the promised Canaan. Happy are the families who are walking hand in hand together, as pilgrims, towards the heavenly country. May the number of such be daily increasing!"

Casting my eye over the numerous dwellings in the vales on the right and left, I could not help thinking, "How many of their inhabitants are ignorant of the ways of God, and strangers to his grace! May this thought stimulate to activity and diligence in the cause of immortal souls! They are precious in God's sight—they ought to be so in ours."

Some pointed and affecting observations to that effect recurred to my mind, as having been made by the young person with whom I had been just conversing. Her mind appeared to be much impressed with the duty of speaking and acting for God "while it is day," conscious that "the night cometh, when no man can work."

Her laudable anxiety on this head was often testified to me afterwards, both by letter and conversation. What she felt herself, in respect to endeavours to do good, she happily communicated to others with whom she corresponded or conversed.

Time would not permit my continuing so long in the enjoyment of these meditations, on this lovely mount of observation, as my heart desired. On my return home I wrote a few lines to the Dairyman's daughter, chiefly dictated by the train of thought which had occupied my mind while I sat on the hill.

On the next Sunday evening I received her reply, of which the following is a transcript:—

"Sunday

Rev. Sir,—

I am this day deprived of an opportunity of attending the house of God to worship Him. But, glory be to his name! He is not confined to time nor place. I feel Him present with me where I am, and his presence makes my paradise; for where He is, is heaven. I pray God that a double portion of his grace and Holy Spirit may rest upon you this day; that his blessing may attend all your faithful labors; and that you may find the truth of his Word, assuring us, that wherever we assemble together in his name, there He is in the midst to bless every waiting soul.

How precious are all his promises! We ought never to doubt the truth of his Word; for He will never deceive us if we go on in faith, always expecting to receive what his goodness waits to give. Dear sir, I have felt it very consoling to read your kind letter to-day. I feel thankful to God for ministers in our Church who love and fear his name; there it is where the people in general look for salvation; and there may they ever find it, for Jesus' sake! May his Word, spoken by you, his chosen vessel of grace, be made spirit and life to their dead souls. May it come from you as an instrument in the hands of God, as sharp arrows from a strong archer, and strike a death-blow to all their sins. How I long to see the arrows of conviction fasten on the minds of those that are hearers of the word and not doers! O, sir! be ambitious for the glory of God and the salvation of souls: it will add to the lustre of your crown in glory, as well as to your present joy and peace. We should be willing to spend and be spent in his service, saying, 'Lord, may thy will be done by me on earth, even as it is by thy angels in heaven.' So you may expect to see his face with joy, and say, 'Here am I, Lord, and all the souls thou hast given me.'

It seems wonderful that we should neglect any opportunity of doing good, when there is, if it be done from love to God and his creatures, a present reward of grace, in reflecting that we are using the talents committed to our care, according to the power and ability which we receive from Him. God requires not what He has not promised to give. But when we look back and reflect that there have been opportunities in which we have neglected to take up our cross, and speak and act for God, what a dejection of mind we feel! We are then justly filled with shame. Conscious of being ashamed of Christ, we cannot come with that holy boldness to a throne of grace, nor feel that free access when we make our supplications.

We are commanded to provoke one another to love and good works; and where two are agreed together in the things of God, they may say:

'And if our fellowship below
In Jesus be so sweet,
What heights of rapture shall we know
When round the throne we meet!'

Sir, I hope Mrs—and you are both of one heart and one mind. Then you will sweetly agree in all things that make for your present and eternal happiness. Christ sent his disciples out, not singly, but two and two, that they might comfort and help each other in those ways and works which their Lord commanded them to pursue.

It has been my lot to have been alone the greatest part of the time that I have known the ways of God. I therefore find it such a treat to my soul when I can meet with any who loves to talk of the goodness and love of God, and all his gracious dealings. What a comfortable reflection, to think of spending a whole eternity in that delightful employment—to tell to listening angels his love, 'immense, unsearchable!'

Dear sir, I thank you for your kindness and condescension in leaving those that are of high rank and birth in the world, to converse with me who am but a servant here below. But when I consider what a high calling, what honor and dignity God has conferred upon me, to be called his child, to be born of his Spirit, made an heir of glory, and joint heir with Christ, how humble and circumspect should I be in all my ways, as a dutiful and loving child to an affectionate and loving Father! When I seriously consider these things, it fills me with love and gratitude to God, and I do not wish for any higher station, nor envy the rich. I rather pity them if they are not good as well as great. My blessed Lord was pleased to appear in the form of a servant, and I long to be like Him.

I did not feel in so happy a frame for conversation that day, nor yet that liberty to explain my thoughts, which I sometimes do. The fault must have been all in myself; for there was nothing in you but what seemed to evidence a Christian spirit, temper, and disposition. I very much wished for an opportunity to converse with you. I feel very thankful to God that you do take up the cross, and despise the shame: if you are found faithful, you will soon sit down with Him in glory.

I have written to the Rev. Mr—, to thank him for permitting you to perform the burial service at—, over my dear departed sister, and to tell him of the kind way in which you consented to do it. I should mention that your manner of reading the service on that day had a considerable effect on the hearers.

Pray excuse all faults, and correct my errors. I expect in a few days to return home to my parent's house. We shall rejoice to see you there.

From your humble servant in Christ,
—Elizabeth Wallbridge"

It was impossible to view such a correspondent with indifference. I had just returned from a little cottage assembly, where, on Sunday evenings, I sometimes went to instruct a few poor families in one of the hamlets belonging to my parish. I read the letter, and closed the day with thanksgiving to God for thus enabling those who fear his name to build up each other in faith and love.

Of old time, "they that feared the Lord spake often one to another: and the Lord hearkened and heard it; and a book of remembrance was written before Him for them that feared the Lord, and that thought upon his name."

That book of remembrance is not yet closed.

CHAPTER THREE

The mind of man is like a moving picture, supplied with objects not only from contemplation on things present, but from the fruitful sources of recollection and anticipation.

Memory retraces past events, and restores an ideal reality to scenes which are gone by forever. They live again in revived imagery, and we seem to hear and see with renewed emotions what we heard and saw at a former period. Successions of such recollected circumstances often form a series of welcome memorials. In religious meditations the memory becomes a sanctified instrument of spiritual improvement.

Another part of this animated picture is furnished by the pencil of Hope. She draws encouraging prospects for the soul, by connecting the past and present with the future. Seeing the promises afar off, she is persuaded of their truth, and embraces them as her own.

The Spirit of God gives a blessing to both these acts of the mind, and employs them in the service of religion. Every faculty of body and soul, when considered as a part of "the purchased possession" of the Savior, assumes a new character. How powerfully does the apostle, on this ground, urge a plea for holy activity and watchfulness! "What! know ye not that your body is the temple of the Holy Ghost which is in you, which ye have of God, and ye are not your own? For ye are bought with a price: therefore glorify God in your body, and in your spirit, which are God's." (1 Cor. 6:19, 20)

The Christian may derive much profit and enjoyment from the use of the memory, as it concerns those transactions in which he once bore a part. In his endeavours to recall past conversations and intercourse with deceased friends in particular, the powers of remembrance greatly improve by exercise. One revived idea produces another, till the mind is most agreeably and usefully occupied with lively and holy imaginations.

"Lull'd in the countless chambers of the brain, Our thoughts are linked by many a hidden chain; Awake but one, and lo, what myriads rise! Each stamps its image as the other flies; Each, as the varied avenues of sense Delight or sorrow to the soul dispense, Brightens or fades: yet all with sacred art Control the latent fibres of the heart."

May it please God to bless, both to the reader and the writer, this feeble attempt to recollect some of the communications I once enjoyed in my visits to the Dairyman's dwelling!

Very soon after the receipt of the last letter, I rode, for the first time, to see the family at their own house. The principal part of the road lay through retired, narrow lanes, beautifully overarched with groves of nut and other trees, which screened the traveller from the rays of the sun, and afforded many interesting objects for admiration in the flowers, shrubs, and young trees which grew upon the high banks on each side of the road. Many grotesque rocks, with little trickling streams of water occasionally breaking out of them, varied the recluse scenery, and produced a romantic and pleasing effect.

Here and there the most distant prospect beyond was observable through gaps and hollow places on the road-side. Lofty hills, with navy signal-posts, obelisks, and lighthouses on their summits, appeared at these intervals; rich cornfields were also visible through some of the open places; and now and then, when the road ascended a hill, the sea, with ships at various distances, was seen. But for the most part shady seclusion, and objects of a more minute and confined nature, gave a character to the journey and invited contemplation.

How much do they lose who are strangers to serious meditation on the wonders and beauties of nature! How gloriously the God of creation shines in his works! Not a tree, or leaf, or flower, not a bird or insect, but it proclaims in glowing language, "God made me."

As I approached the village where the good old Dairyman dwelt, I observed him in a little field, driving his cows before him towards a yard and hovel which adjoined his cottage. I advanced very near him without his observing me, for his sight was dim. On my calling out to him, he started at the sound of my voice, but with much gladness of heart welcomed me, saying, "Bless your heart, sir, I am very glad you are come; we have looked for you every day this week."

The cottage-door opened, and the daughter came out, followed by her aged and infirm mother. The sight of me naturally brought to recollection the grave at which we had before met. Tears of affection mingled with the smile of satisfaction with which I was received by these worthy cottagers. I dismounted, and was conducted through a neat little garden, part of which was shaded by two large overspreading elm trees, to the house. Decency and order were manifest within and without. No excuse was made here, on the score of poverty, for confusion and uncleanliness in the disposal of their little household. Everything wore the aspect of neatness and propriety. On each side of the fire-place stood an old oaken chair, where the venerable parents rested their weary limbs after the day's labor was over. On a shelf in one corner lay two Bibles, with a few religious books and tracts. The little room had two windows; a lovely prospect of hills, woods, and fields appeared through one; the other was more than half obscured by the branches of a vine which was trained across it; between its leaves the sun shone, and cast a cheerful light over the whole place.

"This," thought I, "is a fit residence for piety, peace, and contentment. May I learn a fresh lesson for advancement in each, through the blessing of God, on this visit!"

"Sir," said the daughter, "we are not worthy that you should come under our roof. We take it very kind that you should travel so far to see us."

"My Master," I replied, "came a great deal farther to visit us poor sinners. He left the bosom of his Father, laid aside his glory, and came down to this lower world on a visit of mercy and love; and ought not we, if we profess to follow Him, to bear each other's infirmities, and go about doing good as He did?"

The old man now entered, and joined his wife and daughter in giving me a cordial welcome. Our conversation soon turned to the loss they had so lately sustained. The pious and sensible disposition of the daughter was peculiarly manifested, as well in what she said to her parents as in what she more immediately addressed to myself. I had now a further opportunity of remarking the good sense and agreeable manner which accompanied her expressions of devotedness to God and love to Christ, for the great mercies which He had bestowed upon her. During her residence in different gentlemen's families where she had been in service, she had acquired a superior behaviour and address; but sincere piety rendered her very humble and unassuming in manner and conversation. She seemed anxious to improve the opportunity of my visit to the best purpose for her own and her parents' sake; yet there was nothing of unbecoming forwardness, no self-sufficiency or conceitedness in her conduct. She united the firmness and solicitude of the Christian with the modesty of the female and the dutifulness of the daughter. It was impossible to be in her company, and not observe how truly her temper and conversation adorned the principles which she professed.

I soon discovered how eager and how successful also she had been in her endeavours to bring her father and mother to the knowledge and experience of the truth. This is a lovely feature in the character of a young Christian. If it have pleased God, in the free dispensation of his mercy, to call the child by his grace, while the parent remains still in ignorance and sin, how great is the duty incumbent on that child to do what is possible to promote the conversion of those to whom so much is owing. Happy is it when the ties of grace sanctify those of nature.

The aged couple evidently regarded and spoke of this daughter as their teacher and admonisher in Divine things, while at the same time they received from her every token of filial submission and obedience, testified by continual endeavours to serve and assist them to the utmost of her power in the daily concerns of the household.

The religion of this young woman was of a highly spiritual character, and of no ordinary attainment. Her views of the Divine plan of saving the sinner were clear and scriptural. She spoke much of the joys and sorrows which, in the course of her religious progress, she had experienced; but she was fully sensible that there is far more in real religion than mere occasional transition from one frame of mind and spirits to another. She believed that the experimental acquaintance of the heart with God principally consisted in so living upon Christ by faith, as to aim at living like Him by love. She knew that the love of God toward the sinner, and the path of

duty prescribed to the sinner, are both of an unchange-
able nature. In a believing dependence on the one, and
an affectionate walk in the other, she sought and found
"the peace of God which passeth all understanding;"
"for so He giveth his beloved rest."

She had read but few books besides her Bible; but
these few were excellent in their kind, and she spoke of
their contents as one who knew their value. In addition
to a Bible and Prayer-book, *The Rise and Progress of
Religion in the Soul* by Doddridge, *Life, Walk, and
Triumph of Faith* by Romaine, *The Pilgrim's Progress* by
Bunyan, *An Alarm to the Unconverted* by Alleine, *The
Saint's Everlasting Rest* by Baxter, a hymn-book, and a
few tracts, composed her library.

I observed in her countenance a pale and delicate hue,
which I afterwards found to be a presage of consumption; and the idea then occurred to me that she would
not live very long.

Time passed on swiftly with this interesting family;
and after having partaken of some plain and whole-
some refreshment, and enjoyed a few hours' conversation
with them, I found it was necessary for me to return
homewards. The disposition and character of the parties
may be in some sort ascertained by the expressions at
parting.

"God send you safe home again," said the aged mother,
"and bless the day that brought you to see two poor old
creatures, such as we are, in our trouble and affliction.
Come again, sir, come again when you can; and though
I am a poor ignorant soul, and not fit to talk to such

a gentleman as you, yet my dear child shall speak for me; she is the greatest comfort I have left; and I hope the good Lord will spare her to support my trembling limbs and feeble spirits, till I lie down with my other dear departed kindred in the grave."

"Trust to the Lord," I answered, "and remember his gracious promise: 'Even to your old age I am He; and even to hoary hairs I will carry you.'"

"I thank you, sir," said the daughter, "for your Christian kindness to me and my friends. I believe the blessing of the Lord has attended your visit, and I hope I have experienced it to be so. My dear father and mother will, I am sure, remember it; and I rejoice in the opportunity of seeing so kind a friend under this roof. My Savior has been abundantly good to me in plucking me 'as a brand from the burning,' and showing me the way of life and peace; and I hope it is my heart's desire to live to his glory. But I long to see these dear friends enjoy the power and comfort of religion likewise."

"I think it evident," I replied, "that the promise is fulfilled in their case: 'It shall come to pass, that at evening time it shall be light.'"

"I believe it," she said, "and praise God for the blessed hope."

"Thank Him too, that you have been the happy instrument of bringing them to the light."

"I do, sir; yet, when I think of my own unworthiness and insufficiency, I rejoice with trembling."

"Sir," said the good old man, "I am sure the Lord

will reward you for this kindness. Pray for us, old as we are, and sinners as we have been, that yet He would have mercy upon us at the eleventh hour. Poor Betsy strives much for our sakes, both in body and soul; she works hard all day to save us trouble, and I fear has not strength to support all she does; and then she talks to us, and reads to us, and prays for us, that we may be saved from the wrath to come. Indeed, sir, she is a rare child to us."

"Peace be unto you and all that belong to you!"

"Amen, and thank you, dear sir," was echoed from each tongue.

Thus we parted for that time. My returning meditations were sweet, and, I hope, profitable.

Many other visits were afterwards made by me to this peaceful cottage, and I always found increasing reason to thank God for the intercourse I there enjoyed.

An interval of some length occurred once during that year, in which I had not seen the Dairyman's family. I was reminded of the circumstance by the receipt of the following letter:

"Rev. Sir,

I have been expecting to see or hear from you for a considerable time. Excuse the liberty I take in sending you another letter. I have been confined to the house the greater part of the time since I left—. I took cold that day, and have been worse ever since. I walk out a little on these fine days, but seem to myself to walk very near on the borders of eternity. Glory be to God, it is a very pleasing prospect before me. Though I feel the workings of sin, and am abased, yet Jesus shows his mercy to be mine, and I trust that I am his. At such times:

"My soul would leave this heavy clay
At his transporting word,
Run up with joy the shining way
To meet and prove the Lord.

Fearless of hell and ghastly death,
I'd break through every foe;
The wings of love and arms of faith
Would bear me conqueror through."

My desire is to live every moment to God, that I may through his grace be kept in that heavenly, happy frame of mind that I shall wish for at the hour of death. We cannot live nor die happy without this, and to keep it we must be continually watching and praying: for we have many enemies to disturb our peace. I am so very weak, that now I can go nowhere to any outward means for that help which is so refreshing to my spirit.

I should have been very happy to have heard you last Sunday, when you preached at—: I could not walk so far. I hope the Word spoken by you was made a blessing to many that heard it. It was my earnest prayer to God that it might be so. But, alas! once calling does not awaken many that are in a sound sleep. Yet the voice of God is sometimes very powerful when his ministers speak, when they are influenced by his Holy Spirit, and are simple and sincere in holding forth the Word of Life. Then it will teach us all things, and enlighten our mind, and reveal unto us the hidden things of darkness, and give us out of that Divine treasure 'things new and old.' Resting on God to work in us both to will and to do of his good pleasure, we ought always to work as diligent servants, that know they have a good Master, that will surely not forget their labor of love.

If we could but fix our eyes always on that crown of glory that awaits us in the skies, we should never grow weary in well-doing, but should run with patience, and delight in the work and ways of God, where He appoints us. We should not then, as we too frequently do, suffer these trifling objects here on earth to draw our minds from God, to rob Him of his glory, and our souls of that happiness and comfort which the believer may enjoy amidst outward afflictions. If we thus lived more by faith on the Son of God, we should endeavour to stir up all whom we could to seek after God. We should tell them what He has done for us, and what He would do for them if they truly sought Him. We should show them what a glorious expectation there is for all true believers and sincere seekers.

When our minds are so fixed on God, we are more desirous of glorifying Him, in making known his goodness to us, than the proud rich man is of getting honor to himself. I mourn over my own backwardness to this exercise of duty when I think of God's willingness to save the vilest of the vile, according to the dispensations of his eternal grace and mercy. Oh, how amiable, how lovely does this make that God of love appear to poor sinners, that can view Him as such! How is the soul delighted with such a contemplation! They that have much forgiven, how much they love!

These thoughts have been much on my mind since the death of—. I trust the Lord will pardon me for neglect. I thought it was my duty to speak or write to him; you remember what I said to you respecting it. But I still delayed till a more convenient season. Oh, how I was struck when I heard the Lord had taken him so suddenly! I was filled with sorrow and shame for having neglected what I had so often resolved to do. But now the time of speaking for God to him was over. Hence we see that the Lord's time is the best time. Now the night of death was come upon him; no more work was to be done. If I had done all that lay in my power to proclaim reconciliation by Christ to his soul, whether he had heard or no, I should have been more clear of his blood. But I cannot recall the time that is past, nor him from the grave. Had I known the Lord would have called him so suddenly, how diligent I should have been to warn him of his danger. But it is enough that God shows us what we are to do, and not what He is about to do with us or any of his creatures. Pray, sir, do all you can for the glory of God. The time will soon pass by, and then we shall enter that glorious rest that He hath prepared for them that love Him. I pray God to fill you with that zeal and love which He only can inspire, that you may daily win souls to Christ. May He deliver you from all slavish fear of man, and give you boldness, as He did of old those that were filled with the Holy Ghost and with power!

Remember, Christ hath promised to be with all his faithful ministers to the end of time. The greater dangers and difficulties they are exposed to, the more powerful his assistance. Then, sir, let us fear none but Him. I hope you will pray much for me a poor sinner, that God will perfect his strength in my weakness of body and mind; for without Him I can do nothing. But when I can experience the teaching of that Holy One, I need no other teacher. May the Lord anoint you with the same, and give you every grace of his Holy Spirit, that you may be filled with all the fulness of God; that you may know what is the height and depth, the length and breadth of the love of God in Christ Jesus; that you may be in the hand of the Lord, as a keen archer to draw the bow, while the Lord directs and fastens the arrows of conviction in the hearts of such as are under your ministry!

I sincerely pray that you may be made a blessing to him that has taken the place of the deceased. I have heard that you are fellow-countrymen. I hope you are, however, both as strangers in this world, that have no abiding place, but seek a country out of sight. Pray excuse all faults,

From your humble servant in the bonds of the Gospel of Christ,

—Elizabeth Wallbridge"

When I perused this and other letters, which were at different times written to me by the Dairyman's daughter, I felt that in the person of this interesting correspondent were singularly united the characters of an humble disciple and a faithful monitor. I wished to acknowledge the goodness of God in each of these her capacities.

I sometimes entertain a hope that the last day will unfold the value of these epistolary communications, beyond even any present estimate of their spiritual importance.

CHAPTER FOUR

The translation of sinners "from the power of darkness into the kingdom of God's dear Son," is the joy of Christians and the admiration of angels. Every penitent and pardoned soul is a new witness to the triumphs of the Redeemer over sin, death, and the grave. How great the change that is wrought! The child of wrath becomes a monument of grace—a brand plucked from the burning! "If any man be in Christ, he is a new creature: old things are passed away; behold, all things are become new." How marvellous, how interesting is the spiritual history of each individual believer! He is, like David, "a wonder unto many;" but the greatest wonder of all to himself. Others may doubt whether it be so or not; but to him it is unequivocally proved, that, from first to last, grace alone reigns in the work of his salvation.

The character and privileges of real Christians are beautifully described in the language of our Church, which, when speaking of the objects of Divine favour and compassion, says: "They that be endued with so excellent a benefit of God, be called according to God's purpose in due season; they through grace obey the calling: they be justified freely: they be made sons of God by adoption: they be made like the image of his only-begotten Son, Jesus Christ: they walk religiously in good works; and at length, by God's mercy, they attain to everlasting felicity."

Such a conception and display of the Almighty wisdom, power, and love, is indeed "full of sweet, pleasant, and unspeakable comfort to godly persons, and such as feel in themselves the working of the Spirit of Christ mortifying the works of the flesh, and their earthly members; and drawing up their minds to high and heavenly things: it doth greatly establish and confirm their faith of eternal salvation, to be enjoyed through Christ, and doth fervently kindle their love towards God."

Nearly allied to the consolation of a good hope through grace, as it respects our own personal state before God, is that of seeing its evidences shed lustre over the disposition and conduct of others. Bright was the exhibition of the union between true Christian enjoyment and Christian exertion, in the character whose moral and spiritual features I am attempting to delineate.

It seemed to be the first wish of her heart to prove to others, what God had already proved to her, that Jesus is "the Way, the Truth, and the Life." She desired to evince the reality of her calling, justification, and adoption into the family of God, by showing a conformity to the image of Christ, and by walking "religiously in good works;" she trusted that, in this path of faith and obedience, she should "at length, by God's mercy, attain to everlasting felicity."

I had the spiritual charge of another parish, adjoining to that in which I resided. It was a small district, and had but few inhabitants. The church was pleasantly situated on a rising bank, at the foot of a considerable hill. It was surrounded by trees, and had a rural, retired appearance. Close to the churchyard stood a large old mansion, which had formerly been the residence of an opulent and titled family; but it had long since been appropriated to the use of the estate as a farm-house. Its outward aspect bore considerable remains of ancient grandeur, and gave a pleasing character to the spot of ground on which the church stood.

In every direction the roads that led to this house of God possessed distinct but interesting features. One of them ascended between several rural cottages, from the sea-shore, which adjoined the lower part of the village street. Another winded round the curved sides of the adjacent hill, and was adorned both above and below with numerous sheep, feeding on the herbage on the down. A third road led to the church by a gently rising approach, between high banks, covered with young trees, bushes, ivy, hedge-plants, and wild flowers.

From a point of land which commanded a view of all these several avenues, I used sometimes for a while to watch my congregation gradually assembling together at the hour of Sabbath worship. They were in some directions visible for a considerable distance. Gratifying associations of thought would form in my mind, as I contemplated their approach, and successive arrival within the precincts of the house of prayer.

One day, as I was thus occupied, during a short interval previous to the hour of Divine service, I reflected on the joy which David experienced, at the time he exclaimed: "I was glad when they said unto me, Let us go into the house of the Lord. Our feet shall stand within thy gates, Oh Jerusalem. Jerusalem is builded as a city that is compact together: whither the tribes go up, the tribes of the Lord, unto the testimony of Israel, to give thanks unto the Lord." (Ps. 122:1-4)

I was led to reflect upon the various blessings connected with the establishment of public worship. "How many immortal souls are now gathering together, to perform the all-important work of prayer and praise— to hear the Word of God—to feed upon the Bread of Life! They are leaving their respective dwellings, and will soon be united together in the house of prayer. How beautifully does this represent the effect produced by the voice of 'the Good Shepherd,' calling his sheep from every part of the wilderness into his fold! As these fields, hills, and lanes are now covered with men, women, and children, in various directions, drawing near to each other, and to the object of their journey's end: even so, many 'shall come from the east, and from the west, and from the north, and from the south, and shall sit down in the kingdom of God.'" (Lk. 13:29)

Who can rightly appreciate the value of such hours as these?—hours spent in learning the ways of holy pleas- antness and the paths of heavenly peace—hours devoted to the service of God and of souls; in warning the sinner to flee from the wrath to come; in teaching the ignorant how to live and die; in preaching the Gospel to the poor; in healing the broken-hearted; in declaring "deliverance to the captives, and recovering of sight to the blind." "Blessed is the people that know the joyful sound; they shall walk, Oh Lord, in the light of thy countenance. In thy name shall they rejoice all the day, and in thy righteousness shall they be exalted."

My thoughts then pursued a train of reflection on the importance of the ministerial office, as connected in the purposes of God with the salvation of sinners. I inwardly prayed that those many individuals whom He had given me to instruct, might not, through my neglect or error, be as sheep having no shepherd, nor as the blind led by the blind; but rather that I might, in season and out of season, faithfully proclaim the simple and undisguised truths of the Gospel, to the glory of God and the prosperity of his Church.

At that instant, near the bottom of the inclosed lane which led to the churchyard, I observed a friend, whom, at such a distance from his own home, I little expected to meet. It was the venerable Dairyman. He came up the ascent, leaning with one hand on his trusty staff, and with the other on the arm of a younger man, well known to me, who appeared to be much gratified in meeting with such a companion by the way.

My station was on the top of one of the banks which formed the hollow road beneath. They passed a few yards below me. I was concealed from their sight by a projecting tree. They were talking of the mercies of God, and the unsearchable riches of his grace. The Dairyman was telling his companion what a blessing the Lord had given him in his daughter. His countenance brightened as he named her, and called her his precious Betsy.

I met them at a stile not many yards beyond, and accompanied them to the church, which was hard by.

"Sir," said the old man, "I have brought a letter from my daughter: I hope I am in time for Divine service. Seven miles is now become a long walk for me: I grow old and weak. I am very glad to see you, sir."

"How is your daughter?"

"Very poorly, indeed, sir: very poorly. The doctors say it is a decline. I sometimes hope she will get the better of it; but then again I have many fears. You know, sir, that I have cause to love and prize her. Oh, it would be such a trial; but the Lord knows what is best. Excuse my weakness, sir."

He put a letter into my hand, the perusal of which I reserved till afterwards, as the time was nigh for going into church.

The presence of this aged pilgrim, the peculiar reverence and affection with which he joined in the different parts of the service, excited many gratifying thoughts in my mind; such as rather furthered than interrupted devotion.

The train of reflection in which I had engaged, when I first discovered him on the road, at intervals recurred powerfully to my feelings, as I viewed that very congregation assembled together in the house of God, whose steps, in their approach towards it, I had watched with prayerful emotions.

"Here the rich and poor meet together in mutual acknowledgment, that the Lord is the Maker of them all; that all are alike dependent creatures, looking up to one common Father to supply their wants both temporal and spiritual.

"Again, likewise, will they meet together in the grave, that undistinguished receptacle of the opulent and the needy.

"And once more, at the judgment-seat of Christ, shall the rich and the poor meet together, 'that every one may receive the things done in his body, according to that he hath done, whether it be good or bad.'" (2 Cor. 5:10)

"How closely connected in the history of man are these three periods of a general meeting together!

"The house of prayer—the house appointed for all living—and the house not made with hands eternal in the heavens. May we never separate these ideas from each other, but retain them in a sacred and profitable union! So shall our worshipping assemblies on earth be representatives of the general assembly and Church of the firstborn which are written in heaven."

When the congregation dispersed, I entered into discourse with the Dairyman and a few of the poor of my flock, whose minds were of like disposition to his own. He seldom could speak long together without some reference to his dear child. He loved to tell how merciful his God had been to him, in the dutiful and affectionate attentions of his daughter. All real Christians feel a tender spiritual attachment towards those who have been the instrument of bringing them to an effectual knowledge of the way of salvation: but when that instrument is one so nearly allied, how dear does the relationship become!

If my friend the Dairyman was in any danger of falling into idolatry, his child would have been the idol of his affections. She was the prop and stay of her parents' declining years, and they scarcely knew how sufficiently to testify the gratitude of their hearts, for the comfort and blessing which she was the means of affording them.

While he was relating several particulars of his family history to the others, I opened and read the following letter:—

"Sir,

Once more I take the liberty to trouble you with a few lines. I received your letter with great pleasure, and thank you for it. I am now so weak, that I am unable to walk to any public place of Divine worship: a privilege which has heretofore always so much strengthened and refreshed me. I used to go in anxious expectation to meet my God, and hold sweet communion with Him, and I was seldom disappointed. In the means of grace, all the channels of Divine mercy are open to every heart that is lifted up to receive out of that Divine fullness grace for grace. These are the times of refreshing from the presence of the Lord. How have I rejoiced to hear a faithful and lively messenger, just come, as it were, from communion with God at the throne of grace, with his heart warmed and filled with Divine love, to speak to fallen sinners! Such an one has seemed to me as if his face shone as that of Moses did with the glory of God, when he came down from the mount, where he had been within the veil. May you, sir, imitate him, as he did Christ, that all may see and know that the Lord dwelleth with you, and that you dwell in Him through the unity of the blessed Spirit. I trust you are no stranger to his Divine teaching, aid, and assistance, in all you set your hand to do for the glory of God.

I hope, sir, the sincerity of my wishes for your spiritual welfare will plead an excuse for the freedom of my address to you. I pray the Giver of every perfect gift, that you may experience the mighty workings of his gracious Spirit in your heart and your ministry, and rest your all on the justifying and purifying blood of an expiring Redeemer. Then will you triumph in his strength, and be enabled to say with the poet:

> Shall I through fear of feeble men,
> The Spirit's course strive to restrain?
> Or, undismay'd in deed and word,
> Be a true witness for my Lord?

> Awed by a mortal's frown, shall I
> Conceal the word of God most high!
> How then before Thee shall I dare To stand?
> or, how thine anger bear?

> Shall I, to soothe the unholy throng,
> Soften thy truths and smooth my tongue,
> To gain earth's gilded toys, or flee
> The cross endur'd, my God, by Thee!

> What then is he whose scorn I dread,
> Whose wrath or hate makes me afraid?
> A man! an heir of death! a slave
> To sin! a bubble on the wave!

Yea, let men rage, since Thou wilt spread
Thy shadowing wings around my head:
Since in all pain, thy tender love
Will still my sure refreshment prove.

Still shall the love of Christ constrain
To seek the wand'ring souls of men;
With cries, entreaties, tears to save,
And snatch them from the yawning grave.

For this, let men revile my name,
No cross I shun, I fear no shame:
All hail reproach, and welcome pain,
Only thy terrors, Lord, restrain!'

I trust, sir, that you see what a glorious high calling yours is, and that you are one of those who walk humbly with God, that you may be taught of Him in all things. Persons in your place are messengers of the Most High God. Is it too much to say, they should live like the angels in all holiness, and be filled with love and zeal for men's souls? They are ambassadors in Christ's stead to persuade sinners to be reconciled to God. So that your calling is above that of angels: for they are afterward to minister to the heirs of salvation; but the sinner must be first reconciled to God. And you are called on from day to day to intercede with man as his friend, that you may win souls to Christ. Christ is ascended up on high, to intercede with his Father for guilty sinners, and to plead for them the merits of his death. So that Christ and his faithful ministers, through the operation of the blessed Spirit, are co-workers together. Yet without Him we can do nothing: our strength is his strength, and his is all the glory from first to last.

It is my heart's prayer and desire, sir, that you may, by a living faith, cleave close to that blessed exalted Lamb of God, who died to redeem us from sin—that you may have a sweet communion with Father, Son, and Spirit—that you may sink deep in love and rise high in the life of God. Thus will you have such discoveries of the beauties of Christ and his eternal glory, as will fill your heart with true delight.

If I am not deceived, I wish myself to enjoy his gracious favour, more than all the treasures which earth can afford. I would, in comparison, look upon them with holy disdain, and as not worth an anxious thought, that they may not have power on my heart, to draw or attract it from God, who is worthy of my highest esteem, and of all my affections. It should be our endeavour to set Him always before us, that in all things we may act as in his immediate presence; that we may be filled with that holy fear, so that we may not dare wilfully to sin against Him. We should earnestly entreat the Lord to mortify the power and working of sin and unbelief within, by making Christ appear more and more precious in our eyes, and more dear to our hearts.

It fills my heart with thankful recollections, while I attempt in this weak manner to speak of God's love to man. When I reflect on my past sins and his past mercies, I am assured, that if I had all the gifts of wise men and angels, I could never sufficiently describe my own inward sense of his undeserved love towards me. We can better enjoy these glorious apprehensions in our hearts, than explain them to others. But oh how unworthy of them all are we? Consciousness of my own corruptions keeps me often low; yet faith and desire will easily mount on high, beseeching God that He would, according to the apostle's prayer, fill me with all his communicable fullness, in the gifts and graces of his Spirit; that I may walk well-pleasing before Him, in all holy conversation, perfecting holiness in his fear.

If I err in boldness, sir, pray pardon me; and in your next letter confirm my hope, that you will be my counsellor and guide.

I can only recompense your kindness to me by my prayers, that your own intercourse with God may be abundantly blessed to you and yours. I consider the Savior saying to you, as He did to Peter, 'Lovest them me?' And may your heartfelt experience be compelled to reply, 'Thou knowest all things, and thou knowest that I love thee supremely.' May He have evident marks of it in all your outward actions of love and humanity, in feeding his flock, and in the inward fervour and affection of all your consecrated powers; that you may be zealously engaged in pulling down the strongholds of sin and Satan, and building up his Church, sowing the seeds of righteousness, and praying God to give the increase; that you may not labor for Him in vain, but may see the trees bud and blossom, and bring forth fruit abundantly, to the praise and glory of your heavenly Master. In order to give you encouragement, He says, 'Whosoever converteth a sinner from the error of his way, shall save a soul from death;' and that will increase the brightness of your crown in glory. This hath Christ merited for his faithful ministers.

I hope, sir, you will receive grace to be sincere in reproving sin, wherever you see it. You will find Divine assistance, and all fear and shame will be taken from you. Great peace will be given to you, and wisdom, strength, and courage, according to your work. You will be as Paul: having much learning, you can speak to men in all stations of life, by God's assistance. The fear of offending them will never prevent you, when you consider the glory of God; and man's immortal soul is of more value than his present favour and esteem. In particular, you are in an office wherein you can visit all the sick. Man's extremity is often God's opportunity. In this way you may prove an instrument in his hand to do his work. Although He can work without means, yet his usual way is by means; and I trust you are a chosen vessel unto Him, to prove his name and declare his truth to all men.

Visiting the sick is a strict command, and a duty for every Christian. None can tell what good may be done. I wish it was never neglected, as it too often is. Many think that, if they attend the Church—the minister to preach and the people to hear—their duty is done. But more is required than this. May the Lord stir up the gift that is in his people and ministers, that they may have compassion on their fellow-sinners, that they may never think it too late, but remember that while there is life there is hope.

Once more, I pray, sir, pardon and excuse all my errors in judgment, and the ignorance that this is penned in; and may God bless you in all things, and particularly your friendship to me and my parents. What a comfort is family religion. I do not doubt but this is your desire, as it is mine, to say:

> I and my house will serve the Lord,
> But first obedient to his word
>   I must myself appear:
> By actions, words, and temper show
> That I my heavenly Master know,
>   And serve with heart sincere.
>
> I must the fair example set;
> From those that on my pleasure wait
>   The stumbling-block remove;
> Their duty by my life explain,
> And still in all my works maintain
>   The dignity of love.
>
> Easy to be entreated, mild,
> Quickly appeas'd and reconciled,
>   A follower of my God:

A saint indeed I long to be,
And lead my faithful family
    In the celestial road.

Lord, if thou dost the wish infuse,
A vessel fitted for thy use
    Into thy hands receive:
Work in me both to will and do,
And show them how believers true
    And real Christians live.

With all-sufficient grace supply,
And then I'll come to testify
    The wonders of thy name,
Which saves from sin, the world, and hell,
Its power may every sinner feel,
    And every tongue proclaim!

Cleans'd by the blood of Christ from sin,
I seek my relatives to win,
    And preach their sins forgiven;
Children, and wife, and servants seize,
And through the paths of pleasantness
    Conduct them all to heaven.'

Living so much in a solitary way, books are my compan-
ions; and poetry, which speaks of the love of God and the
mercies of Christ, is very sweet to my mind. This must be
my excuse for troubling you to read verses which others
have written. I have intended, if my declining state of health
permit, to go to—for a few days. I say this, lest you should
call in expectation of seeing me, during any part of next
week. But my dear father and mother, for whose precious
souls I am very anxious, will reap the benefit of your visit
at all events.

From your humble and unworthy servant,
—Elizabeth Wallbridge"

Having read it, I said to the father of my highly valued correspondent:

"I thank you for being the bearer of this letter; your daughter is a kind friend and faithful counsellor to me, as well as to you. Tell her how highly I esteem her friendship, and that I feel truly obliged for the many excellent sentiments which she has here expressed. Give her my blessing, and assure her that the oftener she writes, the more thankful I shall be."

The Dairyman's enlivened eye gleamed with pleasure as I spoke. The praise of his Elizabeth was a string which could not be touched without causing every nerve of his whole frame to vibrate.

His voice half-faltered as he spoke in reply; the tear stood in his eyes; his hand trembled as I pressed it; his heart was full; he could only say, "Sir, a poor old man thanks you for your kindness to him and his family. God bless you, sir; I hope we shall soon see you again."

Thus we parted for that day.

CHAPTER FIVE

It has not infrequently been observed, that when it is the Lord's pleasure to remove any of his faithful followers out of this life at an early period of their course, they make rapid progress in the experience of Divine truth. The fruits of the Spirit ripen fast, as they advance to the close of mortal existence. In particular, they grow in humility, through a deeper sense of inward corruption, and a clearer view of the perfect character of the Savior. Disease and bodily weakness make the thoughts of eternity recur with frequency and power. The great question of their own personal salvation, the quality of their faith, the sincerity of their love, and the purity of their hope, are in continual exercise.

Unseen realities, at such a time, occupy a larger portion of thought than before. The state of existence beyond the grave, the invisible world, the unaltered character of the dead, the future judgment, the total separation from everything earthly, the dissolution of body and spirit, and their reunion at the solemn hour of resurrection—these are subjects for their meditation, which call for serious earnestness of soul. Whatever consolations from the Spirit of God they may have enjoyed heretofore, they become now doubly anxious to examine and prove themselves, "whether they be indeed in the faith." In doing this, they sometimes pass through hidden conflicts of a dark and distressing nature; from which, however, they come forth, like gold tried in the furnace. Awhile they may sow in tears, but soon they reap in joy.

Their religious feelings have then, perhaps, less of ecstasy, but more of serenity.

As the ears of corn ripen for the harvest, they bow their heads nearer to the ground. So it is with believers; they then see more than ever of their own imperfection, and often express their sense of it in strong language; yet they repose with a growing confidence on the love of God through Christ Jesus. The nearer they advance to their eternal rest, the more humble they become, but not the less useful in their sphere. They feel anxiously desirous of improving every talent they possess to the glory of God, knowing that the time is short.

I thought I observed the truth of these remarks fulfilled in the progressive state of mind of the Dairyman's daughter.

Declining health seemed to indicate the will of God concerning her. But her character, conduct, and experience of the Divine favour increased in brightness as the setting sun of her mortal life approached its horizon. The last letter which, with the exception of a very short note, I ever received from her, I shall now transcribe. It appeared to me to bear the marks of a still deeper acquaintance with the workings of her own heart, and a more entire reliance upon the free mercy of God.

The original, while I copy it, strongly revives the image of the deceased, and the many profitable conversations which I once enjoyed in her company and that of her parents. It again endears to me the recollections of cottage piety; and helps me to anticipate the joys of that day when the spirits of the glorified saints shall be reunited to their bodies, and be forever with the Lord.

The writer of this and the preceding letters herself little imagined, when they were penned, that they would ever be submitted to the public eye. That they now are so, results from a conviction that the friends of the pious poor will estimate them according to their value, and a hope that it may please God to honor these memorials of the dead, to the effectual edification of the living.

"Rev. Sir,

In consequence of your kind permission, I take the liberty to trouble you with another of my ill-written letters; and I trust you have too much of your blessed Maker's lowly, meek, and humble mind to be offended with a poor, simple, ignorant creature, whose intentions are pure and sincere in writing. My desire is that I, a weak vessel of his grace, may glorify his name for his goodness towards me. May the Lord direct me by his counsel and wisdom! May He overshadow me with his presence, that I may sit beneath the banner of his love, and find the consolations of his blessed Spirit sweet and refreshing to my soul!

When I feel that I am nothing, and God is all in all, then I can willingly fly to Him, saying, 'Lord, help me; Lord, teach me; be unto me my Prophet, Priest, and King;

let me know the teaching of thy grace, and the disclosing of thy love.' What nearness of access might we have if we lived more near to God! What sweet communion might we have with a God of love! He is the great I AM. How glorious a name! Angels with trembling awe prostrate themselves before Him, and in humble love adore and worship Him. One says,—

'While the first archangel sings,
He hides his face behind his wings.'

Unworthy as I am, I have found it by experience, that the more I see of the greatness and goodness of God, and the nearer union I hope I have had with Him through the Spirit of his love, the more humble and self-abased I have been.

But every day I may say, 'Lord, how little I love thee, how far I live from thee, how little am I like thee in humility!' It is nevertheless my heart's desire to love and serve Him better. I find the way in which God does more particularly bless me, is when I attend on the public ordinances of religion. These are the channels through which He conveys the riches of his grace and precious love to my soul. These I have often found to be indeed the time of refreshing and strengthening from the presence of the Lord. Then I can see my hope of an interest in the covenant of love, and praise Him for his mercy to the greatest of sinners.

I earnestly wish to be more established in the ways, and to honor him in the path of duties whilst I enjoy the smiles of his favour. In the midst of all outward afflictions I pray that I may know Christ, and the power of his resurrection within my soul. If I were always thus, my summer would last all the year, my will would then be sweetly lost in God's will, and I should feel a resignation to every dispensation of his providence and his grace, saying, 'Good is the will of the Lord: infinite wisdom cannot err.' Then would patience have its perfect work.

But, alas! sin and unbelief often, too often, interrupt these frames, and lay me low before God in tears of sorrow. I often think what a happiness it would be, if his love were so fixed in my heart, that I might willingly obey Him with alacrity and delight, and gradually mortify the power of self-will, passion, and pride. This can only arise from a good hope, through grace, that we are washed in that precious blood which cleanses us from every sinful stain, and makes us new creatures in Christ. Oh that we may be the happy witnesses of the saving power and virtue of that healing stream which flow from the fountain of everlasting love!

Sir, my faith is often exceedingly weak. Can you be so kind as to tell me what you have found to be the most effectual means of strengthening it? I often think how plainly the Lord declares—Believe only, and thou shalt be saved. Only have faith; all things are possible to him that has it. How I wish that we could remove all those mountains that hinder and obstruct the light of his grace; so that, having full access unto God through that ever-blessed Spirit, we might lovingly commune with Him as with the dearest of friends. What favour doth God bestow on worms! And yet we love to murmur and complain. He may well say, What should I have done more that I have not done? or wherein have I proved unfaithful or unkind to my faithless backsliding children?

Sir, I pray that I may not grieve Him, as I have done, any more. I want your counsel and your prayers for me in this matter. How refreshing is the sight of one that truly loves God, that bears his image and likeness!

But delightful as is conversation with true believers on earth, whose hearts are lifted up to things above, yet what is this to that happy day which will admit us into more bright realms, where we shall forever behold a God of love in the smiling face of his Son, who is the express image of his Father, and the brightness of his glory! Then, if found in Him, we shall be received by the innumerable host of angels who wait around his throne.

In the meantime, sir, may I take up my cross, and manfully fight under Him who, for the glory that was set before Him, endured the cross, despised the shame, and is now set down at his Father's right hand in majesty! I thank you for the kind liberty you have given to me of writing to you. I feel my health declining, and I find a relief during an hour of pain and weakness in communicating these thoughts to you.

I hope, sir, you go on your way rejoicing; that you are enabled to thank Him who is the giver of every good gift, spiritual, temporal, and providential, for blessings to yourself and your ministry. I do not doubt but you often meet with circumstances which are not pleasing to nature; yet, by the blessing of God, they will be all profitable in the end. They are kindly designed by grace to make and keep us humble. The difficulties which you spoke of to me some time since, will, I trust, disappear.

My dear father and mother are as well as usual in bodily health; and, I hope, grow in grace, and in the knowledge and love of Jesus Christ. My chief desire to live is for their sakes. It now seems long since we have seen you. I am almost ashamed to request you to come to our little cottage, to visit those who are so far beneath your station in life. But if you cannot come, we shall be very glad if you will write a few lines. I ought to make an excuse for my letter, I spell so badly: this was a great neglect when I was young. I gave myself greatly to reading, but not to the other; and now I am too weak and feeble to learn much.

I hear sometimes of persons growing serious in your congregation. It gives me joy; and, if true, I am sure it does so to yourself. I long for the pure Gospel of Christ to be preached in every church in the world, and for the time when all shall know, love, and fear the Lord, and the uniting Spirit of God shall make them of one heart and mind in Christ our great Head. Your greatest joy, I know, will be in laboring much for the glory of God in the salvation of men's souls. You serve a good Master. You have a sure reward. I pray God to give you strength according to your day.

Pray, sir, do not be offended at the freedom and manner of my writing. My parents' duty and love to you are sent with these lines from

Your humble servant in Christ,

—Elizabeth Wallbridge"

Epistolary communications, when written in sincerity of heart, afford genuine portraits of the mind. May the foregoing be viewed with Christian candour, and consecrated to affectionate memory!

CHAPTER SIX

Travellers, as they pass through the country, usually stop to inquire whose are the splendid mansions which they discover among the woods and plains around them. The families, titles, fortune, or character of the respective owners engage much attention. Perhaps their houses are exhibited to the admiring stranger. The elegant rooms, costly furniture, valuable paintings, beautiful gardens and shrubberies, are universally approved; while the rank, fashion, taste, and riches of the possessor, afford ample materials for entertaining discussion. In the meantime, the lowly cottage of the poor husbandman is passed by as scarcely deserving of notice. Yet perchance such a cottage may often contain a treasure of infinitely more value than the sumptuous palace of the rich man; even "the pearl of great price." If this be set in the heart of the poor cottager, it proves a gem of unspeakable worth, and will shine among the brightest ornaments of the Redeemer's crown, in that day when He maketh up his "jewels."

Hence the Christian traveller, while in common with others he bestows his due share of applause on the decorations of the rich, and is not insensible to the beauties and

magnificence which are the lawfully-allowed append-
ages of rank and fortune, cannot overlook the humbler
dwelling of the poor. And if he should find that true piety
and grace beneath the thatched roof which he has in
vain looked for amidst the worldly grandeur of the rich,
he remembers the declarations in the Word of God. He
sees with admiration, that the high and lofty One that
inhabiteth eternity, whose name is Holy, who dwelleth
in the high and holy place, dwelleth with him also that
is of a contrite and humble spirit; and although heaven
is his throne, and the earth his footstool, yet, when a
house is to be built, and a place of rest to be sought for
himself, He says, To this man will I look, even to him
that is poor and of a contrite spirit, and trembleth at my
word. (See Isa. 57:15; 66:1, 2)

When a house is thus tenanted, faith beholds this
inscription written on the walls, The Lord lives here.
Faith, therefore, cannot pass by it unnoticed, but loves to
lift up the latch of the door, and to sit down and converse
with the poor, although perhaps despised, inhabitant.
Many a sweet interview does Faith obtain, when she thus
takes her walks abroad. Many such a sweet interview
have I myself enjoyed beneath the roof where dwelt the
Dairyman and his little family.

I soon perceived that his daughter's health was
rapidly on the decline. The pale, wasting consumption,
which is the Lord's instrument for removing so many
thousands every year from the land of the living, made
hasty strides on her constitution. The hollow eye, the
distressing cough, and the often too-flattering red on

the cheek, foretold the approach of death.

What a field for usefulness and affectionate attention on the part of ministers and Christian friends is opened by the frequent attacks, and lingering progress, of consumptive illness! How many such precious opportunities are daily lost, where Providence seems in so marked a way to afford time and space for serious and godly instruction! Of how many may it be said, "The way of peace have they not known;" for not one friend ever came nigh to warn them to "flee from the wrath to come."

But the Dairyman's daughter was happily made acquainted with the things which belonged to her everlasting peace before the present disease had taken root in her constitution. In my visits to her, I went rather to receive information than to impart it. Her mind was abundantly stored with Divine truths, and her conversation was truly edifying. The recollection of it must ever produce a thankful sensation in my heart.

I one day received a short note to the following effect:—

> "Dear Sir,
>
> I should be very glad, if your convenience will allow, that you would come and see a poor unworthy sinner. My hour-glass is nearly run out; but I hope I can see Christ to be precious to my soul. Your conversation has often been blessed to me, and I now feel the need of it more than ever. My father and my mother send their duty to you.
>
> From your obedient
> And unworthy servant,
> —Elizabeth Wallbridge"

I obeyed the summons that same afternoon. On my arrival at the Dairyman's cottage his wife opened the door. The tears streamed down her cheek as she silently shook her head. Her heart was full. She tried to speak, but could not. I took her by the hand, and said:

"My good friend, all is right, and as the Lord of wisdom and mercy directs."

"Oh! my Betsy, my dear girl, is so bad, sir. What shall I do without her? I thought I should have gone first to the grave, but—"

"But the Lord sees good that, before you die yourself, you should behold your child safe home to glory. Is there no mercy in this?"

"Oh, dear sir! I am very old and very weak, and she is a dear child, the staff and prop of such a poor old creature as I am."

As I advanced, I saw Elizabeth sitting by the fireside, supported in an arm-chair by pillows, with every mark of rapid decline and approaching death. A sweet smile of friendly complacency enlightened her pale countenance as she said:

"This is very kind indeed, sir, to come so soon after I sent to you. You find me daily wasting away, and I cannot have long to continue here. My flesh and my heart fail; but God is the strength of my weak heart, and, I trust, will be my portion forever."

The conversation was occasionally interrupted by her cough and want of breath. Her tone of voice was clear, though feeble; her manner solemn and collected; and her eye, though more dim than formerly, by no means wanting in liveliness as she spoke. I had frequently admired the superior language in which she expressed her ideas, as well as the scriptural consistency with which she communicated her thoughts. She had a good natural understanding; and grace, as is generally the case, much improved it. On the present occasion I could not help thinking she was peculiarly favoured. The whole strength of gracious and natural attainments seemed to be in full exercise.

After taking my seat between the daughter and the mother (the latter fixing her fond eyes upon her child with great anxiety, while we were conversing), I said to Elizabeth:

"I hope you enjoy a sense of the Divine presence, and can rest all upon Him who has 'been with thee,' and has kept 'thee in all places whither thou hast gone,' and will bring thee into 'the land of pure delights, where saints immortal reign.'"

"Sir, I think I can. My mind has lately been sometimes clouded, but I believe it has been partly owing to the great weakness and suffering of my bodily frame, and partly to the envy of my spiritual enemy, who wants to persuade me that Christ has no love for me, and that I have been a self-deceiver."

"And do you give way to his suggestions? Can you doubt amidst such numerous tokens of past and present mercy?"

"No, sir; I mostly am enabled to preserve a clear evidence of his love. I do not wish to add to my other sins that of denying his manifest goodness to my soul.

I would acknowledge it to his praise and glory."

"What is your present view of the state in which you were before you felt seriously concerned about the salvation of your soul?"

"Sir, I was a proud, thoughtless girl, fond of dress and finery; I loved the world, and the things that are in the world; I lived in service among worldly people, and never had the happiness of being in a family where worship was regarded, and the souls of the servants cared for either by master or mistress. I went once on a Sunday to church, more to see and be seen than to pray or hear the word of God. I thought I was quite good enough to be saved, and disliked and often laughed at religious people. I was in great darkness; I knew nothing of the way of salvation; I never prayed, nor was sensible of the awful danger of a prayerless state. I wished to maintain the character of a good servant, and was much lifted up whenever I met with applause. I was tolerably moral and decent in my conduct, from motives of carnal and worldly policy; but I was a stranger to God and Christ; I neglected my soul; and had I died in such a state, hell must, and would justly, have been my portion."

"How long is it since you heard the sermon which you hope, through God's blessing, effected your conversion?"

"About five years ago."

"How was it brought about?"

"It was reported that a Mr—, who was detained by contrary winds from embarking onboard ship, as chaplain to a distant part of the world, was to preach at church. Many advised me not to go, for fear he should turn my head; as they said he held strange notions. But curiosity and an opportunity of appearing in a new gown, which I was very proud of, induced me to ask leave of my mistress to go. Indeed, sir, I had no better motives than vanity and curiosity. Yet thus it pleased the Lord to order it for his own glory.

"I accordingly went to church, and saw a great crowd of people collected together. I often think of the contrary states of my mind during the former and latter part of the service. For a while, regardless of the worship of God, I looked around me, and was anxious to attract notice myself. My dress, like that of too many gay, vain, and silly servant girls, was much above my station, and very different from that which becomes an humble sinner, who has a modest sense of propriety and decency. The state of my mind was visible enough from the foolish finery of my apparel.

"At length the clergyman gave out his text: 'Be ye clothed with humility' (1 Pet. 5:5). He drew a comparison between the clothing of the body with that of the soul. At a very early part of his discourse, I began to feel ashamed of my passion for fine dressing and apparel; but when he came to describe the garment of salvation with which a Christian is clothed, I felt a powerful discovery of the nakedness of my own soul. I saw that I had neither the humility mentioned in the text, nor any one part of the true Christian character. I looked at my gay dress, and blushed for shame on account of my pride. I looked at the minister, and he seemed to be as a messenger sent

from heaven to open my eyes. I looked on the congregation, and wondered whether any one else felt as I did.
I looked at my heart, and it appeared full of iniquity. I
trembled as he spoke, and yet I felt a great drawing of
heart to the words he uttered.

"He displayed the riches of Divine grace in God's
method of saving the sinner. I was astonished at what I
had been doing all the days of my life. He described the
meek, lowly, and humble example of Christ; I felt proud,
lofty, vain, and self-consequential. He represented Christ
as 'Wisdom;' I felt my ignorance. He held Him forth as
'Righteousness;' I was convinced of my own guilt. He
proved Him to be 'Sanctification;' I saw my corruption.
He proclaimed Him as 'Redemption;' I felt my slavery
to sin, and my captivity to Satan. He concluded with
an animated address to sinners, in which he exhorted
them to flee from the wrath to come, to cast off the love
of outward ornaments, to put on Jesus Christ, and be
clothed with true humility.

"From that hour I never lost sight of the value of my
soul, and the danger of a sinful state. I inwardly blessed
God for the sermon, although my mind was in a state
of great confusion.

"The preacher had brought forward the ruling passion
of my heart, which was pride in outward dress; and
by the grace of God it was made instrumental to the
awakening of my soul. Happy, sir, would it be, if many
a poor girl, like myself, were turned from the love of
outward adorning and putting on of fine apparel, to seek
that which is not corruptible, even the ornament of a

meek and quiet spirit, which is in the sight of God of great price.

"The greater part of the congregation, unused to such faithful and scriptural sermons, disliked and complained of the severity of the preacher: while a few, as I afterwards found, like myself, were deeply affected, and earnestly wished to hear him again. But he preached there no more.

"From that time I was led, through a course of private prayer, reading, and meditation, to see my lost estate as a sinner, and the great mercy of God through Jesus Christ in raising sinful dust and ashes to a share in the glorious happiness of heaven. And O, sir, what a Savior I have found! He is more than I could ask or desire. In his fullness I have found all that my poverty could need; in his bosom I have found a resting-place from all sin and sorrow; in his Word I have found strength against doubt and unbelief."

"Were you not soon convinced," I said, "that your salvation must be an act of entire grace on the part of God, wholly independent of your own previous works or deservings?"

"Dear sir, what were my works before I heard that sermon, but evil, carnal, selfish, and ungodly? The thoughts of my heart, from my youth upward, were only evil, and that continually. And my deservings, what were they but the deservings of a fallen, depraved, careless soul, that regarded neither law nor gospel? Yes, sir, I immediately saw that, if ever I were saved, it must be by the free mercy of God, and that the whole praise and honor of the work would be his from first to last."

"What change did you perceive in yourself with respect to the world?"

"It appeared all vanity and vexation of spirit. I found it necessary to my peace of mind to come out from among them and be separate. I gave myself to prayer; and many a happy hour of secret delight I enjoyed in communion with God. Often I mourned over my sins, and sometimes had a great conflict through unbelief, fear, temptation, to return back again to my old ways, and a variety of difficulties which lay in my way. But He who loved me with an everlasting love, drew me by his loving-kindness, showed me the way of peace, gradually strengthened me in my resolutions of leading a new life, and taught me, that while without him I could do nothing, I yet might do all things through his strength."

"Did you not find many difficulties in your situation, owing to your change of principle and practice?"

"Yes, sir, every day of my life. I was laughed at by some, scolded at by others, scorned by enemies, and pitied by friends. I was called hypocrite, saint, false deceiver, and many more names which were meant to render me hateful in the sight of the world. But I esteemed the reproach of the Cross an honor. I forgave and prayed for my persecutors, and remembered how very lately I had acted the same part towards others myself. I thought also that Christ endured the contra-diction of sinners; and as the disciple is not above his Master, I was glad to be in any way conformed to his sufferings."

"Did you not then feel for your family at home?"

"Yes, that I did indeed, sir; they were never out of my thoughts. I prayed continually for them, and had a longing desire to do them good. In particular, I felt for my father and mother, as they were getting into years, and were very ignorant and dark in matters of religion."

"Ay," interrupted her mother, sobbing, "ignorant and dark, sinful and miserable we were, till this dear Betsy—this dear Betsy—this dear child, sir—brought Christ Jesus home to her poor father and mother's house."

"No, dearest mother; say rather, Christ Jesus brought your poor daughter home, to tell you what He had done for her soul, and, I hope, to do the same for yours."

At this moment the Dairyman came in with two pails of milk hanging from the yoke on his shoulders. He had stood behind the half-opened door for a few minutes, and heard the last sentences spoken by his wife and daughter.

"Blessing and mercy upon her!" said he, "it is very true: she left a good place of service on purpose to live with us, that she might help us both in soul and body. Sir, don't she look very ill? I think, sir, we sha'n't have her here long."

"Leave that to the Lord," said Elizabeth. "All our times are in his hand, and happy it is that they are. I am willing to go. Are not you willing, my father, to part with me into his hands who gave me to you at first?"

"Ask me any question in the world but that," said the weeping father.

"I know," said she, "you wish me to be happy."

"I do, I do," answered he; "let the Lord do with you and us as best pleases Him."

I then asked her on what her present consolations chiefly depended, in the prospect of approaching death.

"Entirely, sir, on my view of Christ. When I look at myself, many sins, infirmities, and imperfections cloud the image of Christ which I want to see in my own heart. But when I look at the Savior himself, He is altogether lovely; there is not one spot in his countenance, nor one cloud over all his perfections.

"I think of his coming in the flesh, and it reconciles me to the sufferings of the body; for He had them as well as I. I think of his temptations, and believe that He is able to succor me when I am tempted. Then I think of his cross, and learn to bear my own. I reflect on his death, and long to die unto sin, so that it may no longer have dominion over me. I sometimes think of his resurrection, and trust that He has given me a part in it, for I feel that my affections are set upon things above. Chiefly, I take comfort in thinking of Him as at the right hand of the Father, pleading my cause, and rendering acceptable even my feeble prayers, both for myself, and, as I hope, for my dear friends.

"These are the views which, through mercy, I have of my Savior's goodness; and they have made me wish and strive in my poor way to serve Him, to give myself up to Him, and to labor to do my duty in that state of life into which it has pleased Him to call me.

"A thousand times I should have fallen and fainted, if He had not upheld me. I feel that I am nothing without Him. He is all in all.

"Just so far as I can cast my care upon Him I find strength to do his will. May He give me grace to trust Him till the last moment! I do not fear death, because I believe that He has taken away its sting. And O, what happiness beyond! Tell me, sir, whether you think I am right—I hope I am under no delusion. I dare not look for my hope in anything short of the entire fullness of Christ. When I ask my own heart a question, I am afraid to trust it, for it is treacherous, and has often deceived me. But when I ask Christ, he answers me with promises that strengthen and refresh me, and leave me no room to doubt his power and will to save. I am in his hands, and would remain there; and I do believe that He will never leave nor forsake me, but will perfect the thing that concerns me. He loved me, and gave himself for me; and I believe that his gifts and calling are without repentance. In this hope I live, in this hope I wish to die."

I looked around me, as she was speaking, and thought—Surely this is none other than the house of God, and the gate of heaven. Everything appeared neat, cleanly, and interesting. The afternoon had been rather overcast with dark clouds; but just now the setting sun shone brightly and somewhat suddenly into the room. It was reflected from three or four rows of bright pewter plates and white earthenware, arranged on shelves against the wall; it also gave brilliancy to a few prints of sacred subjects that hung there also, and served for monitors of the birth, baptism, crucifixion, and resurrection of Christ.

A large map of Jerusalem, and a hieroglyphic of "the old and new man," completed the decorations on that side of the room. Clean as was the whitewashed wall, it was not cleaner than the rest of the place and its furniture. Seldom had the sun enlightened a house where order and general neatness (those sure attendants of pious poverty) were more conspicuous.

This gleam of setting sunshine was emblematical of the bright and serene close of this young Christian's departing season. One ray happened to be reflected from a little looking-glass upon her face. Amidst her pallid and decaying features there appeared a calm resignation, triumphant confidence, unaffected humility, and tender anxiety, which fully declared the feelings of her heart.

Some further affectionate conversation and a short prayer closed this interview.

As I rode home by departing day-light, a solemn tranquillity reigned throughout the scene. The gentle lowing of cattle, the bleating of sheep just penned in their folds, the humming of the insects of the night, the distant murmurs of the sea, the last notes of the birds of day, and the first warblings of the nightingale, broke upon the ear, and served rather to increase than lessen the peaceful serenity of the evening, and its corresponding effects on my own mind. It invited and cherished just such meditations as my visit had already inspired. Natural scenery, when viewed in a Christian mirror, frequently affords very beautiful illustrations of Divine truths. We are highly favoured when we can enjoy them, and at the same time draw near to God in them.

CHAPTER SEVEN

It is a pleasing consideration that, amidst the spiritual darkness which unhappily prevails in many parts of the land, God nevertheless has a people. It not infrequently happens, that single individuals are to be found who, though very disadvantageously situated with regard to the ordinary means of grace, have received truly saving impressions, and through a blessing on secret meditation, reading, and prayer, are led to the closest communion with God, and become eminently devoted Christians. It is the no small error of too many professors of the present day, to overlook or undervalue the instances of this kind which exist. The religious profession and opinions of some have too much of mere machinery in their composition. If every wheel, pivot, chain, spring, cog, or pinion, be not exactly in its place, or move not precisely according to a favorite and prescribed system, the whole is rejected as unworthy of regard. But happily "the Lord knoweth them that are his;" nor is the impression of his own seal wanting to characterise some who, in comparative seclusion from the religious world, "name the name of Christ, and depart from iniquity."

There are some real Christians so particularly circumstanced in this respect, as to illustrate the poet's beautiful comparison:—

> "Full many a gem of purest ray serene
> The dark unfathom'd caves of ocean bear;
> Full many a flower is born to blush unseen,
> And waste its sweetness on the desert air."

Yet this was not altogether the case with the Dairyman's daughter. Her religion had indeed ripened in seclusion from the world, and she was intimately known but to few; but she lived usefully, departed most happily, and left a shining track behind her. While I attempt a faint delineation of it, may I catch its influence, and become, through inexpressible mercy, a follower "of them, who through faith and patience inherit the promises."

From the time wherein I visited her, as described in my last paper, I considered her end as fast approaching. One day I received a hasty summons to inform me that she was dying. It was brought by a soldier, whose countenance bespoke seriousness, good sense, and piety.

"I am sent, sir, by the father and mother of Elizabeth Wallbridge, at her own particular request, to say how much they all wish to see you. She is going home, sir, very fast indeed."

"Have you known her long?" I inquired.

"About a month, sir. I love to visit the sick; and hearing of her case from a person who lives close by our camp, I went to see her. I bless God that ever I did go. Her conversation has been very profitable to me."

"I rejoice," said I, "to see in you, as I trust, a brother

soldier. Though we differ in our outward regimentals, I hope we serve under the same spiritual Captain. I will go with you."

My horse was soon ready. My military companion walked by my side, and gratified me with very sensible and pious conversation. He related some remarkable testimonies of the excellent disposition of the Dairyman's daughter, as they appeared from recent intercourse which he had had with her.

"She is a bright diamond, sir," said the soldier, "and will soon shine brighter than any diamond upon earth."

We passed through lanes and fields, over hills and through valleys, by open and retired paths, sometimes crossing over, and sometimes following the windings of a little brook, which gently murmured by the road-side. Conversation beguiled the distance, and shortened the apparent time of our journey, till we were nearly arrived at the Dairyman's cottage.

As we approached it, we became silent. Thoughts of death, eternity, and salvation, inspired by the sight of a house where a dying believer lay, filled my own mind, and, I doubt not, that of my companion also.

No living object yet appeared, except the Dairyman's dog, keeping a kind of mute watch at the door; for he did not, as formerly, bark at my approach. He seemed to partake so far of the feelings appropriate to the circumstances of the family, as not to wish to give a hasty or painful alarm. He came forward to the little wicket-gate, then looked back at the house-door, as if conscious there was sorrow within. It was as if he wanted to say, "Tread softly over the threshold, as you enter the house of mourning; for my master's heart is full of grief."

The soldier took my horse, and tied it up in a shed. A solemn serenity appeared to surround the whole place; it was only interrupted by the breezes passing through the large elm-trees, which stood near the house, and which my imagination indulged itself in thinking were plaintive sighs of sorrow. I gently opened the door; no one appeared; and all was yet silent. The soldier followed; we came to the foot of the stairs.

"They are come," said a voice, which I knew to be the father's "they are come."

He appeared at the top. I gave him my hand, and said nothing. On entering the room above, I saw the aged mother and her son supporting the much-loved sister: the son's wife sat weeping in a window-seat, with a child on her lap; two or three persons attended in the room to discharge any office which friendship or necessity might require.

I sat down by the bed-side. The mother could not weep, but now and then sighed deeply, as she alternately looked at Elizabeth and at me. The big tear rolled down the brother's cheek, and testified an affectionate regard. The good old man stood at the foot of the bed, leaning upon the post, and unable to take his eyes off the child from whom he was so soon to part.

Elizabeth's eyes were closed, and as yet she perceived me not. But over the face, though pale, sunk, and hollow, the peace of God which passeth all understanding, had cast a triumphant calm.

The soldier, after a short pause, silently reached out his Bible towards me, pointing with his finger at 1 Corinthians 15:55, 56, 58. I then broke silence by reading the passage, "Oh death, where is thy sting? Oh grave, where is thy victory? The sting of death is sin, and the strength of sin is the law. But thanks be to God which giveth us the victory through our Lord Jesus Christ."

At the sound of these words her eyes opened, and something like a ray of Divine light beamed on her countenance, as she said, "Victory, victory! through our Lord Jesus Christ."

She relapsed again, taking no further notice of any one present.

"God be praised for the triumph of faith!" said I.

"Amen!" replied the soldier.

The Dairyman's uplifted eye showed that the amen was in his heart, though his tongue failed to utter it. A short struggling for breath took place in the dying young woman, which was soon over; and then I said to her,—

"My dear friend, do you not feel that you are supported?"

"The Lord deals very gently with me," she replied.

"Are not his promises now very precious to you?"

"They are all yea and amen in Christ Jesus."

"Are you in much bodily pain?"

"So little, that I almost forget it."

"How good the Lord is!"

"And how unworthy am I!"

"You are going to see Him as He is."

"I think—I hope—I believe that I am."

She again fell into a short slumber.

Looking at her mother, I said, "What a mercy to have a child so near heaven as yours is!"

"And what a mercy," she replied, in broken accents, "if her poor old mother might but follow her there! But, sir, it is so hard to part!"

"I hope through grace by faith you will soon meet, to part no more: it will be but a little while."

"Sir," said the Dairyman, "that thought supports me, and the Lord's goodness makes me feel more reconciled than I was."

"Father, mother," said the reviving daughter, "He is good to me—trust Him, praise Him evermore."

"Sir," added she, in a faint voice, "I want to thank you for your kindness to me—I want to ask a favour; you buried my sister—will you do the same for me?"

"All shall be as you wish, if God permit;" I replied.

"Thank you, sir, thank you. I have another favour to ask: when I am gone, remember my father and mother. They are old, but I hope the good work is begun in their souls. My prayers are heard. Pray come and see them. I cannot speak much, but I want to speak for their sakes. Sir, remember them."

The aged parents now sighed and sobbed aloud, uttering broken sentences, and gained some relief by such an expression of their feelings.

At length I said to Elizabeth—"Do you experience any doubts or temptations on the subject of your eternal safety?"

"No, sir; the Lord deals very gently with me, and gives me peace."

"What are your views of the dark valley of death, now that you are passing through it?"

"It is not dark."

"Why so?"

"My Lord is there, and He is my light and my salvation."

"Have you any fears of more bodily suffering?"

"The Lord deals so gently with me, I can trust Him."

Something of a convulsion came on. When it was past, she said again and again:

"The Lord deals very gently with me. Lord, I am thine, save me—blessed Jesus—precious Savior—his blood cleanseth from all sin—Who shall separate?—His name is Wonderful—Thanks be to God—He giveth us the victory—I, even I, am saved—Oh grace, mercy, and wonder—Lord, receive my spirit! Dear sir, dear father, mother, friends, I am going—but all is well, well, well—"

She relapsed again. We knelt down to prayer: the Lord was in the midst of us, and blessed us.

She did not again revive while I remained, nor ever speak any more words which could be understood. She slumbered for about ten hours, and at last sweetly fell asleep in the arms of that Lord who had dealt so gently with her.

I left the house an hour after she had ceased to speak. I pressed her hand as I was taking leave, and said "Christ is the Resurrection and the Life." She gently returned the pressure, but could neither open her eyes nor utter a reply.

I never had witnessed a scene so impressive as this before. It completely filled my imagination as I returned home.

"Farewell," thought I, "dear friend, till the morning of an eternal day shall renew our personal intercourse. Thou wast a brand plucked from the burning, that thou mightest become a star shining in the firmament of glory. I have seen thy light and thy good works, and will therefore glorify our Father which is in heaven. I have seen, in thy example, what it is to be a sinner freely saved by grace. I have learned from thee, as in a living mirror, who it is that begins, continues, and ends the work of faith and love. Jesus is all in all: He will and shall be glorified. He won the crown, and alone deserves to wear it. May no one attempt to rob Him of his glory! He saves, and saves to the uttermost. Farewell, dear sister in the Lord! Thy flesh and thy heart may fail; but God is the strength of thy heart, and shall be thy portion forever."

CHAPTER EIGHT

Who can conceive or estimate the nature of that change which the soul of a believer must experience at the moment when, quitting its tabernacle of clay, it suddenly enters into the presence of God? If, even while "we see through a glass darkly," the views of Divine love and wisdom are so delightful to the eye of faith, what must be the glorious vision of God, when seen face to face? If it be so valued a privilege here on earth to enjoy the communion of saints, and to take sweet counsel together with our fellow-travellers towards the heavenly kingdom, what shall we see and know when we finally "come unto Mount Zion, and unto the city of the living God, the heavenly Jerusalem, and to an innumerable company of angels, to the General Assembly and Church of the Firstborn, which are written in heaven, and to God, the Judge of all, and to the spirits of just men made perfect, and to Jesus the Mediator of the New Covenant?" (Heb. 12:22-24.)

If, during the sighs and tears of a mortal pilgrimage, the consolations of the Spirit are so precious, and the hope full of immortality is so animating to the soul, what heart can conceive, or what tongue utter its superior joys, when arrived at that state where sighing and sorrow flee away, and the tears shall be wiped from every eye?

Such ideas were powerfully associated together in my imagination as I travelled onward to the house where, in solemn preparation for the grave, lay the remains of the Dairyman's daughter.

She had breathed her last shortly after the visit related in my former account. Permission was obtained, as before, in the case of her sister, that I should perform the funeral service. Many pleasing yet melancholy thoughts were connected with the fulfilment of this task. I retraced the numerous and important conversations which I had held with her.

But these could now no longer be maintained on earth. I reflected on the interesting and improved nature of Christian friendships, whether formed in palaces or in cottages; and felt thankful that I had so long enjoyed that privilege with the subject of this memoir. I then indulged a selfish sigh for a moment, on thinking that I could no longer hear the great truths of Christianity uttered by one who had drunk so deep of the waters of the river of life; but the rising murmur was checked by the animating thought: "She is gone to eternal rest—could I wish her back again in this vale of tears?"

At that moment the first sound of a tolling bell struck my ear. It proceeded from a village church in the valley directly beneath the ridge of a high hill, over which I had taken my way. It was Elizabeth's funeral knell.

The sound was solemn; and in ascending to the elevated spot over which I rode, it acquired a peculiar tone and character. Tolling at slow and regular intervals (as was customary for a considerable time previous to the hour of burial), the bell, as it were, proclaimed the blessedness of the dead who die in the Lord, and also the necessity of the living pondering these things, and laying them to heart. It seemed to say: "Hear my warning voice, thou son of man. There is but a step between thee and death. Arise, prepare thine house, for thou shall die and not live."

The scenery was in unison with that tranquil frame of mind which is most suitable for holy meditation. A rich and fruitful valley lay immediately beneath; it was adorned with cornfields and pastures through which a small river winded in a variety of directions, and many herds grazed upon its banks. A fine range of opposite hills, covered with grazing flocks, terminated with a bold sweep into the ocean, whose blue waves appeared at a distance beyond. Several villages, hamlets, and churches, were scattered in the valley. The noble mansions of the rich, and the lowly cottages of the poor, added their respective features to the landscape.

Do any of my readers inquire why I describe so minutely the circumstances of prospect and scenery which may be connected with the incidents I relate? My reply is, that the God of redemption is the God of creation likewise; and that we are taught in every part of the Word of God to unite the admiration of the beauties and wonders of nature to every other motive for devotion. When David considered the heavens, the work of God's fingers, the moon and the stars which He has ordained, he was thereby led to the deepest humiliation of heart before his Maker. And when he viewed the sheep, and the oxen, and the beasts of the field, the fowl of the air, and the fish of the sea, he was constrained to cry out, "Oh Lord, our Lord, how excellent is thy name in all the earth!" (Ps. 8:1)

I am the poor man's friend, and wish more especially that every poor laboring man should know how to connect the goodness of God in creation and providence, with the unsearchable riches of his grace in the salvation of a sinner. And where can he learn this lesson more instructively than in looking around the fields, where his labor is appointed, and there tracing the handiwork of God in all that he beholds? Such meditations have often afforded me both profit and pleasure, and I wish my readers to share them with me.

The Dairyman's cottage was rather more than a mile distant from the church. A lane, quite overshadowed with trees and high hedges, led from the foot of the hill to his dwelling. It was impossible at that time to overlook the suitable gloom of such an approach to the house of mourning.

I found, on my entrance, that several Christian friends from different parts of the neighbourhood had assembled together, to pay their last tribute of esteem and regard to the memory of the Dairyman's daughter. Several of them had first become acquainted with her during the latter stage of her illness: some few had maintained an affectionate intercourse with her for a longer period. But all seemed anxious to manifest their respect for one who was endeared to them by such striking testimonies of true Christianity.

I was requested to go into the chamber where the relatives and a few other friends were gone to take a last look at the remains of Elizabeth.

It is not easy to describe the sensation which the mind experiences on the first sight of a dead countenance, which, when living, was loved and esteemed for the sake of that soul which used to give it animation. A deep and awful view of the separation that has taken place between the soul and body of the deceased, since we last beheld them, occupies the feelings; our friend seems to be both near, and yet far off. The most interesting and valuable part is fled away: what remains is but the earthly perishing habitation, no longer occupied by its tenant. Yet the features present the accustomed association of friendly intercourse. For one moment we could think them asleep. The next reminds us that the blood circulates no more: the eye has lost its power of seeing, the ear of hearing, the heart of throbbing, and the limbs of moving. Quickly a thought of glory breaks in upon the mind, and we imagine the dear departed soul to be arrived at its long wished-for rest. It is surrounded by cherubim and seraphim, and sings the song of Moses and the Lamb on Mount Zion. Amid the solemn stillness of the chamber of death, imagination hears heavenly hymns chanted by the spirits of just men made perfect. In another moment, the livid lips and sunken eye of the clay-cold corpse recall our thoughts to earth, and to ourselves again. And while we think of mortality, sin, death, and the grave, we feel the prayer rise in our bosom—"O let me die the death of the righteous, and let my last end be like his!"

If there be a moment when Christ and salvation, death, judgment, heaven, and hell, appear more than ever to be momentous subjects of meditation, it is that which brings us to the side of a coffin containing the body of a departed believer.

Elizabeth's features were altered, but much of her likeness remained. Her father and mother sat at the head, her brother at the foot of the coffin. The father silently and alternately looked upon his dead child, and then lifted up his eyes to heaven. A struggle for resignation to the will of God was manifest in his countenance; while the tears rolling down his aged cheeks at the same time declared his grief and affection. The poor mother cried and sobbed aloud, and appeared to be much overcome by the shock of separation from a daughter so justly dear to her. The weakness and infirmity of old age added a character to her sorrow, which called for much tenderness and compassion.

A remarkably decent-looking woman, who had the management of the few simple though solemn ceremonies which the case required, advanced towards me, saying:

"Sir, this is rather a sight of joy than of sorrow. Our dear friend Elizabeth finds it to be so, I have no doubt. She is beyond all sorrow. Do you not think she is, sir?"

"After what I have known, and seen, and heard," I replied, "I feel the fullest assurance that while her body remains here, the soul is with her Savior in Paradise. She loved Him here, and there she enjoys the pleasures which are at his right hand forevermore."

"Mercy, mercy upon a poor old creature, almost broken down with age and grief! What shall I do? Betsy's gone! My daughter's dead! O, my child! I shall never see thee more! God be merciful to me a sinner!"—sobbed out the poor mother.

"That last prayer, my dear, good woman," said I, "will bring you and your child together again. It is a cry that has brought thousands to glory. It brought your daughter there, and I hope it will bring you thither likewise. God will in nowise cast out any that come to Him."

"My dear," said the Dairyman, breaking the long silence he had maintained, "let us trust God with our child; and let us trust Him with our ownselves. 'The Lord gave, and the Lord hath taken away; blessed be the name of the Lord!' We are old, and can have but a little further to travel in our journey, and then—" he could say no more.

The soldier, mentioned in my last paper, reached a Bible into my hand, and said—"Perhaps, sir, you would not object to reading a chapter before we go to the church?"

I did so; it was the fourteenth of the Book of Job. A sweet tranquillity prevailed while I read it. Each minute that was spent in this funereal chamber seemed to be valuable. I made a few observations on the chapter, and connected them with the case of our departed sister.

"I am but a poor soldier," said our military friend, "and have nothing of this world's goods beyond my daily subsistence; but I would not exchange my hope of salvation in the next world for all that this world could bestow without it. What is wealth without grace? Blessed be God! as I march about from one quarter to another, I still find the Lord wherever I go; and, thanks be to his holy name, He is here to-day in the midst of this company of the living and the dead. I feel that it is good to be here."

Some other persons present began to take a part in our conversation, in the course of which the life and experience of the Dairyman's daughter were brought forward in a very interesting manner. Each friend had something to relate in testimony of her gracious disposition. A young woman under twenty, who had hitherto been a very light and trifling character, appeared to be remarkably impressed by the conversation of that day; and I have since had reason to believe that Divine grace then began to influence her in the choice of that better part, which shall not be taken from her.

What a contrast does such a scene as this exhibit, when compared with the dull, formal, unedifying, and often indecent manner in which funeral parties assemble in the house of death!

As we conversed, the parents revived. Our subject of discourse was delightful to their hearts. Their child seemed almost to be alive again, while we talked of her. Tearful smiles often brightened their countenances, as they heard the voice of friendship uttering their daughter's praises; or rather the praises of Him who had made her a vessel of mercy, and an instrument of spiritual good to her family.

The time for departing was now at hand.

I went to take my last look at the deceased. There was much written on her countenance. She had evidently died with a smile. It still remained, and spoke the tranquillity of her soul. According to the custom of the country, she was decorated with leaves and flowers in the coffin: she seemed as a bride gone forth to meet the bridegroom. These, indeed, were fading flowers, but they reminded me of that paradise whose flowers are immortal, and where her never-dying soul is at rest.

I remembered the last words which I had heard her speak, and was instantly struck with the happy thought that "death was indeed swallowed up in victory."

As I slowly retired, I said inwardly, "Peace, my honored sister, be to thy memory and to my soul, till we meet in a better world."

In a little time, the procession formed: it was rendered the more interesting by the consideration of so many that followed the coffin being persons of a devout and spiritual character. The distance was rather more than a mile. I resolved to continue with and go before them, as they moved slowly onwards.

Immediately after the body came the venerable father and mother,[1] bending with age, and weeping through much affection of heart. Their appearance was calculated to excite every emotion of pity, love, and esteem. The other relatives followed them in order, and the several attendant friends took their places behind.

After we had advanced about a hundred yards, my meditation was unexpectedly and most agreeably interrupted, by the friends who attended beginning to sing a funeral psalm. Nothing could be more sweet or solemn. The well-known effect of the open air, in softening and blending the sounds of music, was here peculiarly felt. The road through which we passed was beautiful and romantic. It lay at the foot of a hill, which occasionally re-echoed the voices of the singers, and seemed to give faint replies to the notes of the mourners. The funeral-knell was distinctly heard from the church tower, and increased the effect which this simple and becoming service produced.

We went by several cottages; a respectful attention was universally observed as we passed: and the countenances of many proclaimed their regard for the departed young woman. The singing was regularly continued, with occasional intervals of about five minutes, during our whole progress.

I cannot describe the state of my own mind as peculiarly connected with this solemn singing. I never witnessed a similar instance before or since. I was reminded of elder times and ancient piety. I wished the practice more frequent. It seems well calculated to excite and cherish devotion and religious affections.

Music, when judiciously brought into the service of religion, is one of the most delightful, and not least efficacious means of grace. I pretend not too minutely to conjecture as to the actual nature of those pleasures which, after the resurrection, the reunited body and soul will enjoy in heaven; but I can hardly persuade myself that melody and harmony will be wanting, when even the sense of hearing shall itself be glorified.

We arrived at the church. The service was heard with deep and affectionate attention. When we came to the grave, the hymn which Elizabeth had selected was sung. All was devout, simple, animating. We committed our dear sister's body to the earth, in full hope of a joyful resurrection.

Thus was the veil of separation drawn for a season. She is departed, and no more seen, but she will be seen on the right hand of her Redeemer at the last day; and will again appear to his glory, a miracle of grace and a monument of mercy.

My reader, rich or poor, shall you and I appear there likewise? Are we "clothed with humility," and arrayed in the wedding-garment of a Redeemer's righteousness? Are we turned from idols to serve the living God? Are we sensible of our own emptiness, and therefore flying to a Savior's fullness to obtain grace and strength? Do we indeed live in Christ, and on Him, and by Him, and with Him? Is He our all in all? Are we "lost and found," "dead and alive again?"

My poor reader, the Dairyman's daughter was a poor girl, and the child of a poor man. Herein thou resemblest her; but dost thou resemble her as she resembled Christ? Art thou made rich by faith? Hast thou a crown laid up for thee? Is thine heart set upon heavenly riches? If not, read this story once more, and then pray earnestly for like precious faith?

But if, through grace, thou dost love and serve the Redeemer that saved the Dairyman's daughter, grace, peace, and mercy be with thee! The lines are fallen unto thee in pleasant places! thou hast a goodly heritage. Press forward in duty, and wait upon the Lord, possessing thy soul in holy patience. Thou hast just been with me to the grave of a departed believer. Now, "go thy way, till the end be; for thou shalt rest, and stand in thy lot at the end of the days."

ENDNOTES

1 An interesting account of a visit made to the Dairyman, appeared in the Christian Guardian for October 1813, and which is here inserted:—

"It has rarely, if ever, fallen to my lot to trace the gracious dealing of God with greater advantage or delight, than in the narrative of the Dairyman's Daughter: and as the Isle of Wight had evidently furnished the author with the scenery he has so finely touched, I concluded that the pious subject of the little memoir had resided there, and determined that, when I next visited that delightful spot, I would make inquiry respecting her. At the close of April last year, I had occasion to go there. At the village of Brading I had the good fortune to learn her name, and the location of the cottage that had been honored with her residence and death; and being told that the old man, her father, whose name is Wallbridge, still lived there, I determined to find out his humble dwelling, and obtain an interview with the aged Dairyman.

It was with feelings not to be described that I visited the spot which had been so peculiarly honored by the gracious presence of the Most High. On inquiry, I found that Elizabeth Wallbridge died about eleven years ago; that her mother followed her in the same year; that one of her brothers (whom I did not see) lived in the same cottage; and that her father was about eighty years of age. The venerable old man appeared to wonder at the feelings of a stranger, but seemed thankful for my visit, and wept as I made past scenes again pass before his view. I was happy to find that his hopes were built upon the Rock of Ages; that his sure trust was in the Redeemer of sinners. We talked of the kind attentions of the Rev. Mr. Legh Richmond, of the happy death of Elizabeth, of the wondrous grace of God; and when I bade him farewell, and reminded him how soon he would again see his daughter, not, indeed, encompassed with infirmity, and depressed with disease, but "shining as the sun in the firmament," the poor old man wept plentifully, and little would he be to be envied who could have refrained. I looked back on the cottage until it could no longer be seen, and then went on my way rejoicing.

On the third of November last, being again in that district, I had the pleasure of repeating my visit to the good old Dairyman, who immediately recollected me. He told me many persons had been to see him since my former call, but he believed they were strangers, not inhabitants of the island. He appeared much weaker than before, and evidently drawing nearer to his rest. Whether he is still living, I know not; but it is probable I shall see him no more."

The pious old Dairyman lived three years after this visit: he departed in the hope of meeting his gracious Redeemer.

THE MISSION OF GREAT CHRISTIAN BOOKS

The ministry of Great Christian Books was established to glorify The Lord Jesus Christ and to be used by Him to expand and edify the kingdom of God while we occupy and anticipate Christ's glorious return. Great Christian Books will seek to accomplish this mission by publishing Gospel literature which is biblically faithful, relevant, and practically applicable to many of the serious spiritual needs of mankind upon the beginning of this new millennium. To do so we will always seek to boldly incorporate the truths of Scripture, especially those which were largely articulated as a body of theology during the Protestant Reformation of the sixteenth century and ensuing years. We gladly join our voice in the proclamations of— Scripture Alone, Faith Alone, Grace Alone, Christ Alone, and God's Glory Alone!

Our ministry seeks the blessing of our God as we seek His face to both confirm and support our labors for Him. Our prayers for this work can be summarized by two verses from the Book of Psalms:

"...let the beauty of the LORD our God be upon us, And establish the work of our hands for us; Yes, establish the work of our hands." —Psalm 90:17

"Not unto us, O LORD, not unto us, but to your name give glory." —Psalm 115:1

Great Christian Books appreciates the financial support of anyone who shares our burden and vision for publishing literature which combines sound Bible doctrine and practical exhortation in an age when too few so-called "Christian" publications do the same. We thank you in advance for any assistance you can give us in our labors to fulfill this important mission. May God bless you.

For a catalog of other great
Christian books including
additional titles by
Legh Richmond
contact us in
any of the following ways:

write us at:
Great Christian Books
160 37th Street
Lindenhurst, NY 11757

call us at:
631. 956. 0998

find us online:
www.greatchristianbooks.com

email us at:
mail@greatchristianbooks.com

Printed in Great Britain
by Amazon